Occupations and Society

STUDENTS LIBRARY OF SOCIOLOGY

GENERAL EDITOR: ROY EMERSON

Professor of Sociology
University of East Anglia

Occupations and Society

DAVID DUNKERLEY

Department of Sociology
The University of Leeds

Routledge & Kegan Paul

London and Boston

First published in 1975
by Routledge & Kegan Paul Ltd
Broadway House, 68-74 Carter Lane,
London EC4V 5EL and
9 Park Street,
Boston, Mass. 02108, USA
Set in Linotype Pilgrim
and printed in Great Britain by
Northumberland Press Limited, Gateshead

ISBN 0 7100 8239 8 (c)
      0 7100 8240 1 (p)

Contents

CONTENTS

I

Introduction

The sociology of occupations owes its existence to the fact that work in any society is both a socially desired activity and is ubiquitous. Both of these factors make occupations and more specifically the work that is performed by occupations of central concern to the sociologist. The sociologist views work in terms of the social relationships that are created by it. Since work is a socially desired activity in industrialized societies, it is understandable that it should be viewed as fundamental to understanding social behaviour.

However, occupations are something that are beyond a mere description of work tasks within a particular society. Essentially, occupations are roles within society that are defined by the nature of the work that individuals perform. It follows therefore, as Hughes (1958) has argued, that any occupation may be studied sociologically as long as the criterion of individuals working and being members of an occupation is subscribed to. There would be no sociological significance in analysing an occupation if nobody was employed in it at the present time, had been in the past or was likely to be in the future. But if there is employment of individuals in a given sphere of activity, then that activity has a sociological relevance.

From this straightforward position relating to area of interest, all the components of the sociology of occupations follow. In the first instance, it is important to recognize the achieved nature of occupational and work status in the majority of cases in industrialized societies. It is rare to find ascribed occupational status in industrialized societies. The chapters in this book reflect the kinds of questions that we ask once these essential points are recognized. Thus, accepting the notion of achieved social role as fundamental to occupations leads us to ask questions as to why individuals choose one occupation rather than another and to explore the social constraints placed upon individuals in this choice process. Once in an occupation we can ask about the nature of movement within that occupation and what comprises an occupational career.

Occupations themselves vary in the degree of cohesion they display and the extent of control that they can exercise over their members: again such issues are of sociological interest. Related to the notions of cohesion and control is the amount of status and prestige conferred upon the occupation. As a special category of occupational status, the professions can be distinguished and these require a separate discussion because of their unusual characteristics vis-à-vis other occupations. A further area covered by this volume concerns the influence that the occupation has upon the lives of its members, not only while the individual is at work, but also in the non-work sphere of activity—at home, in the community and in leisure pursuits.

Each of these areas of interest arises from the sociological approach to the study of occupations, an approach which rests upon the assumption of work roles being social roles as well.

The actual status of occupational sociology within the general discipline of sociology is ambiguous. Traditionally, it has been viewed as a part of industrial sociology, at other times as part of the sociology of organizations, and yet again as a part of economic sociology. Only in comparatively recent years has it been possible to see the emergence of the field as a distinctive area of analysis in its own right.

It is perhaps strange that the field should have taken so long to develop a separate identity in the light of how many studies have been conducted almost from the beginning of sociology itself. The names of 'founding fathers' in sociology such as Marx, Durkheim and Weber are all familiar to the occupational sociologist. At a less theoretical level, the work of many of the early American sociologists is associated with the field, particularly that work emanating from the University of Chicago in the first half of this century.

How recent the development of the field is can be illustrated by the fact that one of the foremost writers on occupational sociology, writing in 1954, argued that the field developed accidentally and certainly as a peripheral interest to those most concerned with social institutions such as the family, the army or the church. Indeed, Caplow goes on to argue that at the time he was writing occupational sociology did not have a specific and unique identity as a field of study. Admittedly his book *The Sociology of Work* is an attempt to develop such an identity and yet Caplow has difficulty even in trying to define an occupation. Whilst, as here, Caplow discusses the nature of the social role that is associated with the work an individual does, this is clearly an inadequate kind of definition of occupation. Similarly in discussing the notion of a societal division of labour and the variations in the assignment of work with the development of society, these discussions do not provide definitions. All of this tends to indicate that two decades ago the field was not capable of exact definition or even strict delineation. What this volume shows is that the sociology of occupations has progressed in that time to the stage where it can be taken as an important and distinctive branch of the general discipline of sociology.

The above proposition can be illustrated by reference to what Caplow saw as the two most important questions confronting the sociologist in any discussion of occupations in industrialized societies. First, he was concerned with the ways in which the occupational institution enables society to maintain continuity and existence. Second, the question of what roles are actually created by the occupational institution and how these affect individual behaviour (Caplow, 1954, p. 18).

An exploration of possible answers to the first of these questions necessarily involves a consideration of the way in which societies solve the general problem of production. In spite of the great advances in technology and automation, even the most advanced industrial society must needs use human energies and human skills in order to produce the goods and provide the services that can contribute to the material satisfaction of the individual. The question needs to be asked therefore, how is it that the correct number of people are doing the right things at any particular time? Also, how is it that the learned skills are transmitted from one generation to another for the purposes of continuity? And lastly, how does it occur that what is learned is additive in the sense that change of an improving or progressive kind can be brought about? It would seem, therefore, that there are three basic questions that need to be asked that revolve around the dimensions of structure, culture and change.

3

In relation to the second question posed by Caplow, pursuit of possible answers leads to a wide range of questions and so some attempt at classifying them has to be made. In the first instance, in looking at the roles created, the role of the individual occupation-incumbent could be examined. Normally, it is the case that the roles of employers and employees, or of manual workers and white collar workers, or of independent professionals and wage earners are examined. In fact any broad category that seems to have some meaning for social order can be examined.

In addition, it is necessary to look at the rather special roles that arise from the interdependence of the activities involved in other roles. Such special roles have a close relationship to the mechanisms of co-ordination between occupations. Typical of such roles would be managers, senior professionals and most roles which are dependent upon co-ordinator roles, though not necessarily being of this type themselves.

Finally, concerned with the second question, attention needs to be paid to the way in which occupations accommodate or are accommodated by social differences such as age or sex and by other social institutions such as the family or religion. A large number of questions arise from this perspective that concern the relationship between the worlds of work and non-work. How are skills transmitted from one generation to another? How does the occupation enable the individual to pursue a career? What consequences has the non-work life of the individual for the occupation? And what consequences has the occupation for the individual's non-work life? Who, from a behavioural point of view, are the people attracted to and accepted by the occupation and how do they differ from those who are not? The range of questions is thus very wide. In brief, it can be said that the sociology of occupations is concerned with using occupations as the basic site for sociological investigation and operates on this site with the same sort of tools as those used more widely and generally by sociologists with similar sorts of purposes.

2

Occupational visibility and choice

In any industrial society the majority of individuals have to make the choice of entering into some kind of employment situation. It is normally possible to discern a threshold between the non-work period and the work period of an individual's life. As the previous chapter has suggested, the sociologist distinguishes rather more than the fact that an individual has entered gainful employment: this employment is classified by the type of industry (as seen by the type of end-product of the work process) and by the occupation (as seen by the specific character of the work task). Since, as has already been seen, there are both a large number of industrial and occupational settings in an industrial society and since movement towards a work situation can be classified in either or both of these ways, it means that the assumption can be made that those individuals who cross the threshold from non-work life to work life undertake a choice between those alternatives that theoretically, at least, are open to them.

In this way, it can be argued that the individual who becomes a bus driver has chosen this occupation rather than the occupation of train driver or lorry driver. Of course, the actual range of occupations that are open to him is probably restricted by a variety of factors ranging from the current labour market situation to the individual's own abilities. But this restriction is rarely so extreme that the individual can be said to be in a 'no-choice' situation. In this sense, the notion of a threshold from non-work to work provides a useful introduction and framework for analysing occupational choice.

In a sense, to talk of a threshold is to simplify matters too much.

5

It would be rare for this to be the actual case. Typically, there are a number of stages that have to be passed before it can be said that an actual choice has occurred. Take for example, the schema presented by Miller and Form (1951). They distinguish five stages in the actual process of occupational choice and career development. Admittedly, their process is one which is applicable to the whole of an individual's life, but it is useful as a classification of the adjustments that need to be made.

The five periods in the pattern are preparatory, initial, trial, stable and retirement. Clearly, the first three are most appropriate in the analysis of occupational choice. Each of the periods has a definite set of activities associated with it and in which the individual engages and in which he has to make adjustments. The first and last periods are really non-work periods, thus, the preparatory period is associated with the 'early experiences and adjustments in the home, school and community as the young person develops physical and mental maturity' while the retirement period demands 'new adjustments in the home and community as the work position in the market place is relinquished' (p. 535). Nevertheless, the three definite work periods call for work adjustments that occur in the home and community as well as in the work situation itself. It is instructive to examine these periods in more detail.

The preparatory work period

Through the experiences of family life the child undergoes the socialization process that the sociological and social psychological literature refers to. Part of this learning process involves learning how to adopt and to take on roles. Specifically these are learnt from parents and from contacts in school and friendship groups. The process, therefore, is shared between the family and the school contexts with the former being dominant earlier than the latter.

The influence of the school context is important since part of the educational function in industrial societies is to train the child to meet the expectations of the family, and more especially of the middle class family. Thus, the child is introduced to patterns of authority outside the family context, it operates in a competitive environment, personality and character are developed as are certain social skills. But more than this, in the context of the school the child first comes into contact with a complex organization, with secondary relationships and with actions based more upon rationality than upon spontaneity. In this sense, it is clear how important the school is as a preparation for the world of work.

Furthermore, at the preparatory stage of development for work the child is able to develop a perspective of approach to certain work tasks. While the nature of the rewards at this stage are undoubtedly different from those of the real work situation, certain habits and customs are created at this stage which have an influence on future activities in the work situation. And so it can be argued that the preparatory work period enables the individual to acquire certain skills and perspectives that normally ensure a relatively smooth transition to paid employment. The extent of the success of this phase in developing these skills and perspectives in the individual depends upon factors such as social class, the degree of family cohesion and personality characteristics.

The initial work period

This period is characterized by the individual 'trying out' some of the skills and perspectives acquired through socialization in an actual work situation. Normally this period is characterized by a variety of unskilled and temporary jobs ranging from newspaper rounds and Saturday employment to summer employment.

At this stage can be seen an amalgam of family, educational and work experiences. It follows that the longer period of time that is spent in educational involvement, then the longer it will be before the trial work period comes into play. For those in this situation, the initial work period may act as a functional substitute for the trial work period, although it is generally true that those who continue their education into their late teens or early twenties have a wider range of occupations of an 'initial' kind than do those who complete their education at the minimum leaving age.

A central feature of the initial work period is the amount of independence the child acquires during it in that he becomes less and less dependent upon the home and the family. Miller and Form have suggested that at this stage certain features of the normative structure of the culture are inculcated into the individual. So, at this stage the norms which are culturally determined and regarded as desirable such as learning to accept responsibility, learning the value of money, learning to work hard and so on are transmitted to the individual.

It has been pointed out that while the initial work period experiences can help to mould an individual's personality such social-ization does not always occur as it is designed to. So, for example, the value of learning to accept responsibility can only really be acquired when in a position of responsibility—a situation that is unlikely to pertain at the initial period. For most of the cultural values that Miller and Form suggest are in-built into this period, there are certain contradictions associated with them, particularly in terms of their realization. The result of this situation may be a degree of role conflict for the individual in that certain tensions are created by the irreconcilable contradictions. While it may be argued that this role conflict may be sufficient for anyone to have to deal with there is the added confusion for the individual of the possibility of 'culture shock' and a level of 'marginality' never previously experienced. This may occur since the individual is forced to move from one social and cultural system in a relatively short space of time while at the same time he is only partially acceptable to his new work-mates and to his old school-mates—in any case he is certainly not a full member of either group.

The trial work period

While the two previous work periods may be regarded as some-what transitional, the trial work period marks the introduction of an element of permanence into the work life of the individual. Nevertheless, it is still somewhat transitional in that the individual is at this stage still seeking a truly permanent position. Indeed, Miller and Form estimate that this period may only last for a matter of months. Nevertheless, it is permanent in that it does indicate a complete break from non-work life.

At this time, then, there may be some changing of occupations. Only after the individual has surveyed some or all of the potential alternatives does this period come to an end. In some ways, the individual may often feel himself to be in only temporary employ-ment, preparing himself for a more permanent position or a more responsible job.

It was noted that certain tensions can be generated during the initial work period, but such tensions become more intense during the trial work period. It is at this stage that the individual has to accommodate to a new culture and one whose values are normally not in accord with those of the family, the school or the com-munity. The occupational frustration which occurs at this stage which has been observed by Miller and Form is certainly to be expected and should not in any way be regarded as unusual or pathological. A clear example of occupational frustration arises from the fact that the educational system in most industrialized societies stresses the greater opportunities that are possible. And certainly, the educational system produces many educated and trained people who could command highly paid positions in society. However, their numbers in relation to the actual opportunities that are available have had the tendency to devalue the status of occupations that are normally reached by this route.

As argued later in this volume the emphasis placed upon the value of work has tended to shift in industrialized societies such that the extrinsic rather than the intrinsic value is now stressed. Furthermore, there is increasing evidence to suggest that the derivation of satisfaction from work itself tends to be denied to the individual. Now with such a change of emphasis the coveted occupational goals of an industrial society increasingly become those of high status and high income. But merely because these have become highly valued goals does not mean to say that their achievement is any easier. It is precisely during the trial work period that the individual comes to learn this. If little else, it does reflect the large gap there is between the culture of the family, the school and the community and the culture of the work situation in modern society.

The stable and retired work periods

These two periods are grouped together for the present purposes since they do not reflect directly on occupational choice. The stable work period is so named because of its characteristic security in that at this time the individual has found a job and work situation in which he intends to remain. But it should not be assumed that the term stable automatically means that there will be no shifting of occupation or employment until retirement age, nor that this period is without its own peculiar strains and tensions for the individual. It is during this period that the concept of 'career' is most appropriately applied as discussed in the next chapter. Individual careers are as prone to tension as much as and sometimes more than at any other period of working life.

Unless death occurs, the individual is finally faced with the necessity of retiring from active participation in work. In the retired work period very specific adjustments are called for such as adjusting to the non-work situation, the probability of having a reduced income and the likelihood of lower social status than when in employment.

From the point of view of the discussion of occupational choice it is the first three of these work periods that are deemed important and relevant. During these the main choices are in fact made in terms of bringing the individual into the occupational world, prior to embarking on the stages of a career proper.

The notion of choosing

The use of the term 'occupational choice' implies, by definition, that the coming together of an individual and an occupation has a certain rationality about it. It is undoubtedly true that there is a false implication here for many people, in that when asked why they are employed in a particular position and not in another, it is common for them to respond that they achieved their present position by accident. That is, that little or no rationality was employed by them and that the term choice of occupation appears to be meaningless. For the individual this may well be true, but for the sociologist interested in studying recruitment to occupations there is a certain significance in this. This individual 'accident' can normally be explained in sociological terms and from a sociological perspective, once elements of the social structure, individual social background, and so on are examined. It becomes clear to the sociologist that the term 'accident' may well be inappropriate and that there may be as much determinism in this situation as in the situation where the individual can claim to have made a rational decision about his occupation. What is clear about any individual entering any occupation is that this act is goal-oriented. In order to ensure that the goal is achieved then certain stages of a choice process can be distinguished. In the first instance there has to be a definition of the problem for until this occurs there can be no action to solve it. The problem may be very simply stated to mean the difference between what the position is at the present time from the position as desired at some time in the future. Having defined the problem then the alternative means of solving the problem are next explored. In practice when it comes to a choice of occupation it is probably the case that the majority of people only examine a small proportion of the total number of alternatives presented to them. Once the alternative means have been established a comparison of outcomes is normally made, usually in terms of comparing the career prospects of various occupations and thereby attempting to compare the probable outcome of one course of action with another. Then the actual choice is made and here individual judgment is required in deciding between the possible outcomes that have already been delineated. And finally comes the actual implementation of the decision. With this is an accompanying analysis of the reality with the suspected outcome of an earlier stage.

If decision making can be said to include such sequential elements then it follows that the process of occupational choice necessarily involves certain irreversible, but usually minor, decisions. Once these decisions are made, whether they are the decision to study arts-based rather than science-based subjects at school or whatever, they successively restrict the range of future choices and at some point, for many people, the opportunity to choose any further is terminated. Ginsberg (1951), for example, has described the process of occupational choice as one ending in compromise. The problem with this is that compromise depends on there being a distinction between the choice which is actually made as the result of a series of adaptations to certain situations and the choice which an individual would make if it were possible to decide on a completely 'fresh start' principle.

Katz and Martin (1962) have propounded this view in a study of nurses. As they see it, 'the decisions which underlie embarkation on a nursing career for *at least some persons* revolve around limited situational contingencies—in which the matter of nursing-as-career enters only tangentially or not at all' (pp. 149-50). If this observation is generally true then it follows that it is difficult to separate out those choices which are specifically orientated towards a career from those choices which have to do more with other immediate adaptations to situations as they arise. In other words, since any person is carried along on many dimensions, each of which is interacting with others, it is difficult to plot a single dimension's choice process.

In spite of the difficulties that are inherent in viewing occupational choice in processual terms, various attempts have been made to separate out the different phases in the process. The attempts tend to cluster into two main types, first, the nature of occupational choice as it is related to the maturation of the individual and second, the actual behavioural outcome of the choice itself.

The maturational perspective can be illustrated by Ginsberg's study (1951). Here the process of occupational choice was divided into three periods: fantasy choice (from early childhood to puberty); tentative choice (early adolescence); and realistic choice.

1 The fantasy period: this period has been described in terms of the child's desires and thoughts about adult life. While it is possibly true that these thoughts are determined largely by what is visible to the child, it needs to be stressed that they need not relate to reality in any way, particularly since there is no urgency about making a realistic choice. The roles adopted by children such as doctor, nurse, cowboy or train-driver are therefore a combination of perceived pleasurable roles and also roles that are visible. So it is that occupations such as bank-clerk or assembly-line worker are not role played. Characteristically, the roles that are acted out are both stereotyped and stylized.

It would be unrealistic to suggest that there is a definite relationship between fantasy choices and the realistic choice. It may be that a doctor's son may act out the role of doctor during the fantasy period and may perhaps become a doctor in due course, but this is more likely to be a reflection of the persistence of visibility and parental advice than the influence of the fantasy period upon the ultimate decision.

2 The tentative period: during this period a great deal of realism enters into the choice situation. However, this realism relates to the individual's own desires and aspirations and not necessarily with the position of the labour market. What is significant about this period is the fact that the individual accepts that there is a problem of deciding upon a future occupation, but it must be stressed that any decision which is made is necessarily tentative because of the individual's tenuous relationship with future action at this stage of development and the fact that these choices tend to have more of a symbolic value than a real value.

Ginsberg has sub-divided this period of tentative choice into the stages of (i) interest, (ii) capacity, (iii) value, and (iv) transition. These sub-divisions have the function of highlighting the general themes which influence occupational aspiration at this stage and are self-explanatory.

3 The realistic period: here a choice is made with the definite aim of realizing it in fact. During this period the individual often has to compromise between his own understanding of himself and

his capabilities, interests and so on, and the actual opportunities that are afforded by the environment. So, realizability becomes a crucial factor at this stage, whereas in previous stages it was visibility that was dominant.

As with the previous period, it is possible to break the period down into specific sub-stages, viz.: (i) exploration; (ii) crystallization; and (iii) specification. Each of these sub-stages entails the individual compromising with the real situation, so that the last can be seen to involve specialization and planning within a particular occupational field. A certain crystallization of choice occurs at all ages for many people, but when it does actually occur the individual can definitely be said to have entered the realistic period. But arriving there depends upon a constellation of factors such as the possession of special individual talents or abilities. It can be suggested that such possession is likely to lead to an early emotional commitment to an occupation.

Now, this view of occupational choice is entirely consistent with the many propositions that can be advanced about the sources of influence upon the individual in making occupational choices. Such a view would tend to see the problem in more sociological terms and it is to these that we can now turn.

The social determinants of occupational choice

Up to this point the analysis of occupational choice has tended to focus on theoretical frameworks rather than on specific empirical evidence relating to what actually happens in the choice process. For some time, sociologists have been examining these factors in the process itself, concentrating in particular on the socio-cultural determinants. The word determinants is well chosen for these characteristics tend to be those in the external environment of the individual which suggest that he has little or no control over them. Therefore, such a view of occupational choice is rather deterministic, although the factors already discussed do introduce a degree of individual freedom into the situation. What is important to note though is that these socially determined factors act as limiters and constraints within which the individual then has to make his choice.

As with the analysis of many sociological variables, social class plays an important part in the choosing of an occupation. Other factors that will be considered are sex, type of community and race.

1 Class Culture—The social class culture from which an individual comes is possibly the most important external factor affecting his choice of occupation. The proposition that there is a direct relationship between class level and aspiration level is empirically well-backed. It can be confidently stated that the higher the social class level from which an individual comes, the greater the probability that he will aspire to those occupations that society has defined as the most socially prestigious and economically rewarding. The emphasis here is upon the values that an individual holds and of course associated with this, the motivation to achieve for the individual.

A good empirical example of this relationship comes from a study by the American National Opinion Research Center (NORC). Data were obtained from almost 34,000 graduating students at 135 American universities and colleges (Davis, 1964). In order to illustrate the point being made here the data showing the relationship between family income, father's occupation and education and the student's plans for graduate study (which of course enhances the chances of subsequently obtaining a more prestigious and financially rewarding occupation) can be discussed. In the first instance it was shown that there is the relationship between family status and plans for further study. A similar positive relationship was found between these plans and the rating of the father's occupation. For example, of those whose father's occupation could be classified as 'professional' 38.5 per cent of them had plans for further study, compared with 21.8 per cent of those whose fathers were farmers. And similarly, with father's education, the relationship between this and plans for further study was strongly positive. Taking these three dimensions, it is clear that family background in terms of social class plays a key role in occupational aspirations.

Taking further data from the same study it is clear that there is a relationship between family class background and the types of subjects being pursued by students at a graduate level. The importance of this relationship is that certain subjects provide graduates an entrée into specifically highly rewarded occupations (both socially and economically). Thus, the NORC study provides evidence to the effect that a greater percentage of students from high status family backgrounds studied disciplines such as law and medicine (around 70 per cent) while in the fields of engineering or education the percentage dropped to around 44 per cent having a high status family background.

Another study which sheds light on this relationship between social class and occupational choice is that of Simpson and Simpson (1962). They have suggested that three factors of significance influence individuals when it comes to occupational choice. First, there is the general level of upward mobility within a particular society and the fact that there is a great deal of inheritance of occupational level. Second, the fact that when it comes to the actual choice, many people are greatly influenced by those immediately around them. And lastly, there is the question of the values that people hold with respect to certain occupations. Clearly, these three factors are not mutually exclusive, but display a high level of overlap. In making the NORC findings rather more sophisticated, Simpson and Simpson found that the relationship of occupational advice to status level of first job was independent of the individual's class background among other people with negative work values: it did not seem to matter what the work values were, since if they received a lot of advice from outside the family, they would obtain high-ranking occupations. Similarly, the relationship of occupational values to first job level was independent of advice among workers from white collar family backgrounds: here it did not seem to matter what advice white collar background people received, for if they had positive work values they would achieve high status first jobs more consistently.

2 Sex—In most industrialized societies it is generally true that the occupational aspirations of women are lower than those of men. While this position may be changing quite rapidly in many Western societies, the generality does hold at the present time. The main reason for this lower level of aspiration is to be found in the prevailing cultural ethos with respect to both sex roles and work roles. While it is true that a male's social status is largely determined by his occupation and that there is a predominant cultural norm which stresses the importance of work for men, in the case of females there is not the same normative expectation concerning work. Traditional values stressing the role of the woman in the home whether as wife or mother still prevail, although there is acceptance of economic activity by women. As for the question of status, it is still rare for a woman's occupation to determine her social status absolutely, the husband's occupation is still the crucial thing.

Nevertheless, women comprise approximately one-third of the labour force in the UK. Of this proportion, around two-thirds of them are married, which accounts for the fact that about half of them are part-time workers. While there is this sizeable proportion of females in the labour force, it would be unreal to suggest that except for a minority of them, the general principles of occupational choice as already distinguished in fact apply. The basic reasoning for this is that women tend to be drawn by semi- and unskilled positions on a much larger scale than men. Parker *et al.* (1972) have estimated that only about 5 per cent of employed females are in managerial positions. For the majority of employed females there is the prospect of the work task being made increasingly more routine, since female jobs seem to predominate in those occupations particularly subject to technological change.

But what of occupational choice for females? In the first instance it is still true that the range of occupations for women is relatively narrow which of course restricts the potential choice opportunity. Second, the factor of role priority between the occupational role and the domestic role is important here. If a young girl, for example, has the intention of marrying early in life and raising a family early, then the motivation for undertaking any lengthy training or education will be low. Again, this restricts the range of occupations from which a choice can be made. Third, when the motivations for working of married women are examined (and bear in mind that this group comprises two-thirds of the female work-force) the evidence suggests that money is the chief motivator. Now, this may not be unlike the motivation for working of the majority of the working population, but what is different about married women is that money is seen as instrumental towards a higher standard of living for the family or for certain domestic extras. It is relatively rare for the married woman's wage to be used to provide for the basic sustenance of the household group. Other motives for working include the fact that working does provide an escape from the routine of household chores and simultaneously the potential opportunity for primary relations in the work group. It follows that if such factors are important motivators for women to enter the workforce, then the factor of occupational choice needs to be considered as something rather different from that already discussed. The idea of a process of choice, for example, would seem to be largely inapplicable, since working is much more opportunistic in this instance.

3 Type of Community—In discussing the role played by the community on the individual's choice of occupation, it is usual to distinguish the polar types of the highly rural and highly urban communities. It is well established that the aspirations of individuals in these two polar extremes vary considerably and that the variance is largely due to the varying opportunities for employment that present themselves. So it is that in the urban situation there are more possibilities for a wider range of occupations from which the individual can choose. But more than just having a wider range, it is easier for the individual to become acquainted with these possibilities in the urban situation than it is in the rural one. Sociological research in the past has further suggested that the consequence of this is that individuals in the urban situation are likely to have higher aspiration levels than their counterparts in the rural situation.

The argument therefore seems to hinge on the factor of the visibility of certain occupations. The anecdotal approach of suggesting that, for example, the Welsh have produced proportionately more doctors, teachers and clergymen would support such reasoning, since these are visible occupations in relatively closed communities. But the extent to which these arguments hold today is highly questionable. In terms of visibility, for example, a much wider range of occupations presents itself to most individuals, whether in a rural or urban situation, if only because of the influence of the mass media. The suggestion is, then, that differences in occupational aspiration between urban and rural areas are much less significant than they have been in the past.

Nevertheless, the distinction made between type of community is an important one, but only when the emphasis shifts from stressing visibility of occupation to stressing the opportunities for entering different occupations. For this reason it would seem preferable to use the terms open and closed communities rather than urban and rural respectively. In this way the factor of opportunity to choose from a range of occupations becomes far more relevant.

As an example of the closed situation, a study of the opportunities for employment in the Swansea area of South Wales can be briefly examined (Brennan, Cooney and Pollins, 1954). At the time of the study the mining industry in the area still accounted for 19 per cent and metal manufacture (mainly tin-plate) for 22.5 per cent of local employment. Two points can be made about these figures. First, that these basic heavy industries were important in determining the overall standard of living in the area and second, that little opportunity was afforded for the employment of women. While their general study was concerned with the influence of predominant industries upon labour relations and the general social pattern of the community, it is clear from such a situation that if one or two industries do have such an impact upon an area in terms of employment then other occupations will not be available, thus restricting the opportunities for individuals to pursue them. If there are relatively fewer types of jobs available then the opportunity for the individual to identify with them is likely to be small. Furthermore, in such a situation, there tend to be social pressures placed upon the individual to stay within the community and to pursue similar occupations to his forebears. This has been amply demonstrated in the case of the mining industry (see for example, Dennis *et al.*, 1962; Dunkerley and Mercer, 1974). While more occupations may be visible to the individual, the rather geographically isolated position of many mining communities and the social pressure upon the individual prevent a wide range of occupations presenting themselves from which a choice may be made.

At the other extreme to this is the open type of community. Clearly, not all employment regions or communities are restricted in the number of opportunities provided, or the number that are visible. In the open situation, characterized by urbanism and higher geographical and social mobility, the number of occupations occurring to the individual is likely to be much greater than in most of the stereotypical mining communities that have been alluded to so far. In the open situation there is a tendency for individuals entering occupations to aspire to higher levels of status as denoted by the occupation than in the previous generation. Parallel to this higher status aspiration there is the possibility of aspiring to a higher occupational skill level. In sum, what is often referred to as the industrial caste system of the more closed community situation is broken down in the open situation so that different factors are brought to bear on the choice situation. While it may still be true that a variety of background factors influence occupational choice in the open situation from which it is difficult for the individual to escape, the major difference is that in the closed situation many of these circumstances are defined by occupational titles. In the more open situation the circumstances tend to be defined more by status-grade titles.

4 Race—That race acts as a constraint on occupational choice is very clear from the position of racial minorities in Britain. While it is generally accepted that a major reason for large scale immigration to this country of Asians and West Indians in the late 1950s and early 1960s was the search for employment, it is interesting to note the kinds of employment situation these immigrants have largely found themselves in. It can be assumed that aspirations were high, but that choice was severely restricted. In spite of anti-discrimination legislation immigrant labour is still drawn towards the nationalized industries, particularly transport and the health service. In private industry, it seems to be the wool and light engineering industries that have been the major employers of immigrant labour. Part of the reason for this restricted range of occupational opportunities undoubtedly has lain in the past in a degree of discrimination as the 1969 report of the Institute of Race Relations has suggested (Rose, 1969). Other reasons also include the low level of skill of immigrants when they arrive in the host country and the desire for employment at all costs. But when the second generation effect is taken into consideration, such explanations are no longer as valid in seeking to explain the reduced range of choices of occupation.

American studies provide some useful clues as to the influence of race in occupational choice. Generally, it has been found that the aspiration levels of whites are higher than those of negroes, regardless of socio-economic background (for example, Holloway and Berreman, 1959; Sprey, 1962). Thus, there is a greater chance of negroes aspiring to manual occupations than their white counterparts; while the white individuals have a greater aspiration towards more white-collar and professional occupations.

Occupational constraints on choice

Until now the discussion has centred around occupational choice and the factors external to the occupation that might limit the nature and the degree of choice. In addition, it is relevant to discuss the position that often occurs where certain occupations set limits upon the entry of individuals into the occupation. As will be shown in a later chapter such limitations are a common feature of the professions and semi-professions. In this case the educational system and the attainment of specific educational attainments comprise the main limits. However, in certain manual occupations a similar procedure can be seen to be present, thereby restricting occupational choice. In the case of manual occupations, the normal constraint is a limitation on the age at which the individual may embark upon the occupation. In effect, this imposes a trial work period upon the individual, but not of a voluntary kind. Internal and external constraints upon entry may be distinguished. An internal constraint is one that is imposed by the nature of the work being done; whereas an external constraint is a demand placed upon the individual entering the occupation by someone or something external to the occupation.

As an example of an occupation having such constraints, Hollowell's study of lorry drivers can be cited (Hollowell, 1968). In the case of lorry driving the internal constraints comprise features such as the nature of the job itself which makes heavy demands upon the individual, the fact that lorry driving often means a great deal of time in isolation from other people, and also the rather limited opportunities to move from one category of driving to another (say, from local haulage to long distance transport).

Similarly there are external constraints which include the legal constraints concerning the driving of different categories of vehicle and the social constraints which implicitly place some obligations on young men to remain in or near their family of origin for a period of time. Admittedly this is a rather nebulous constraint but it is very real in some cases.

Constraints such as these have been shown by Hollowell to place upon the individual a period of around six years between leaving school and entering lorry driving proper, even though the occupations undertaken during this period may have some relevance to lorry driving. These constraints also reveal a high level of commitment to lorry driving on the part of the individual.

If the occupation of lorry driving is compared with other occupations found in the closed community situation, then obvious differences pertain. In the case of the coal miner, the dock worker or the deep-sea fisherman the community generally supports the occupation in the sense that the individual is orientated towards the occupation from an early age and also in the sense that there exist certain community mechanisms to protect leisure-time behaviour. For example, Tunstall (1962) has shown how the fishing community gives the individual fisherman a licence to drink and enjoy himself when on shore in a way that would not normally be tolerated by other communities. In the case of occupations such as lorry driving there is not this kind of support. There may be family and community pressures to prevent the individual embarking on a driving career; such pressures are likely to increase when the driver wishes to change to long distance runs. Furthermore, there is a built-in isolation in the lorry driver's job which may be reinforced and exaggerated by the isolation in both family and community terms.

It is important to recognize, therefore, that the occupation may impose severe constraints upon the individual. Such constraints and limitations certainly limit the potential range of choice of occupation for many individuals, even though the occupation is carried out in a relatively open situation.

Conclusions

This chapter highlights the difficulties confronting the sociologist in attempting to account for and explain any complex phenomenon. Generalizations are difficult because of the heterogeneity of the subject matter. Yet generalizations are a necessary by-product of any theory. Indeed, this is part of the purpose of theory. The subject of occupational choice as surveyed in this chapter displays a wide range of theories, most of which, fortunately, are compatible with one another. Whether occupational choice is seen as a process as the American theorists suggest, or as being subject to the contextual constraints as much of the British material emphasizes, does provide useful explanations of individual behaviour and enable a degree of prediction. The recent debate concerning occupational choice (Williams, 1974) reinforces the point about the difficulties of providing a universally applicable theory. While it could be argued that there are deficiencies in most of the explanations, taken together a reasonably comprehensive picture does emerge. Furthermore, it is a refreshing sign that considerable empirical research has been and is currently being undertaken in this area.

3

Occupational mobility and career

Many academic disciplines have to come to terms with the fact that the language that they use in a very specific sense is often used in an everyday sense too. This latter sense is in many cases evaluative and sometimes even pejorative. There are many instances that can be cited in sociology of this difficulty. Words and concepts such as bureaucracy, alienation and profession have a very special and exact meaning to the sociologist, normally very different from the meaning of the everyday world. The concept of a career is another such term, in that evaluations are often made of the term which the sociologist would not normally make. For example, the term 'career woman' is a common enough expression implying that a woman who devotes herself to her work automatically denies certain commitments which it is felt should be directed towards her family and domestic situation. As another example, when in everyday life we refer to someone putting his career first, there is the assumption that that person is being unnecessarily selfish and is disregarding other important aspects of his life, more often than not at the expense of others.

An initial discussion of career as a sociological concept therefore has to provide a strict meaning which distinguishes it from other evaluative meanings. As a structural concept career must include a related series of jobs which is to a large extent predictable. Furthermore, it is normally the case that this predictable series is arranged in a hierarchy of status. Viewing career in this structural sense means that it is possible to discuss the career of an individual as he passes through the related jobs and the career of a particular occupation, in that most occupations comprise a related series of jobs arranged in status hierarchies.

Confusion from everyday terminology goes further than already suggested. It would be invalid to suggest that the notion of career is solely applicable in the case of non-manual occupations, particularly the professions. Hollowell's study of the lorry driver discussed in the previous chapter indicates quite clearly that a status hierarchy exists in this occupation. Using Hollowell's terms, a typical driving career pattern involves moving from local and small shunting to tramping, then trunking and finally back to shunting. A clear pattern of related jobs within the one occupation can thus be seen, and these are related by a status hierarchy. For the sociologist, therefore, it makes as much sense to discuss the career of the lorry driver as it does to discuss a medical career for a doctor. In our everyday discourse, we would tend not to draw these parallels.

To some extent the example of lorry driving to illustrate the appropriateness of the concept of career for manual occupations is slightly untypical. The example does display an important point, that career patterns are most visible in those occupations (manual or otherwise) where the occupational structures and institutions are the strongest. The point of untypicality is thereby understood, since many, if not most, manual occupations do not have either a strong occupational structure or institution associated with them. Coupled with these characteristics is the further observation that if an occupation does display a definite career pattern for its incumbents, then this is likely to ensure a degree of predictability for both the individual and the occupation and of course a certain associated stability.

It is clear, then, that the notion of a career embraces a number of factors which are not associated merely with the idea of work. Work tends only to symbolize an individual's activity at the present; career suggests a patterned sequence of future activities which in most cases encompass the whole of an individual's working life.

It is normally functional for an occupation to have a structured career system associated with it. If it is known that there can be a progression through several stages of an occupation, then this certainly provides a strong incentive for the individual to remain in that occupation. For the occupation, this establishes a measure of stability within it which can affect the functions that it performs for the individual (for example, the formation of a strong occupational asociation can have several functions ranging from educational to protective). But fixed career points can have dys-functional consequences in that they can lead to a certain rigidity in individual behaviour. Merton (1952) in discussing the relation-ship between bureaucratic structures and individual behaviour has made the point that while a career system within a bureaucratic organization should contribute to the overall efficiency of the enter-prise, certain organizational members may, as a consequence, pursue individual goals rather than the organizational objectives. A further dysfunction of a strict career system within an occupation or organ-ization is that individual initiative and ambition may be restricted, since it may appear to the individual that promotion through the occupational career system is at an automatic level.

The work of Miller and Form has been discussed in the previous chapter. In their earlier work (Form and Miller, 1949) they dis-tinguished the three phases of initial, trial and stable work periods from an analysis of 276 American occupational case histories. These periods enabled a profile of secure and insecure work patterns to be devised. Each of the secure patterns resulted in the stable work period, whereas insecure patterns were associated with rarely reach-ing this period. Analysis indicated that secure work patterns were typical of white collar occupations, apart from clerks who dis-played less security and stability than skilled workers and foremen. Semi- and unskilled workers displayed the greatest degree of in-stability and insecurity in their work lives as measured by pro-gression through the stages discussed above.

Other findings from the study were that once an individual embarked upon a career at a particular occupational level, the probability was that he remained at that level. In terms of the social background effects, Form and Miller found a strong associa-tion between this and subsequent career. Those from a white collar background tended to remain at this level in their careers; those from a manual background either remained at that level or dropped in terms of occupational status. Later chapters will show that this is not a consistent finding, but Form and Miller's work does provide some useful generalizations and framework for further analysis.

There is a disadvantage in construing careers in the way that Form and Miller have done. One conclusion to be drawn from the work is that occupational careers are not experienced by the majority of individuals within society since there is such a great deal of job changing. The point that seems to be missed is that while job changing may go on at a fairly high rate, for most individuals the change of job is little more than a change of employer, it is not really a change of occupation. For example, in Form and Miller's classification, a teacher changing from one school to another (possibly to raise himself in the occupational hierarchy) would be classified in relatively insecure terms, whereas in fact he is marking out a very secure and strong career for himself, while changing employers, but not occupation. In fact, among some professional groups the notion of employer-changing almost seems to have normative undertones. That is, it is both expected and quite normal for professionals to change their employers from time to time, thus enabling movement through the occupational hierarchy.

Merely distinguishing that careers exist in a variety of occupations other than the professions is not sufficient for an understanding of the importance of careers to individuals. The assumption in the discussion so far is that career in various occupations is largely an automatic process which is determined by formal stages, with specific internal and external constraints. In this it has been argued that the notion of career is as applicable to manual occupations such as lorry driving as it is to professional occupations such as medicine. In both cases there are formally defined constraints for admission to the occupation and specific stages in career development.

A large number of cases exist, however, where there are not specifically defined stages in the career process, even though the idea of a career is totally appropriate. In such cases, it has been observed that progression through a career, that is movement from one career stage to another, is very much associated with informal factors bearing upon the occupation and the individual in that occupation.

A good example of this situation is to be found in the case of management. Most occupational sociologists would agree that the occupation of management can constitute a career for its members. Clearly, there are different occupational grades ranging perhaps from foreman and middle management through to senior management positions. Yet, because of the nature of management as an occupation it is difficult to specify the formal requirements that are necessary for an individual to pass from one level in the occupation to another. It can be suggested that informal factors play a significant role here in that they supplement the formal factors that seem to be largely absent.

A study of middle management careers in America by Melvin Dalton (1951) provides a good example. The research site was one factory so there are obvious problems of generalizations, even though the findings are of interest and relevance to the present discussion. Most of the managers in the plant who were Catholics or Protestant non-masons felt that being a member of a masonic order was essential for promotion within the factory. Similarly, it was found that certain ethnic groups had an advantage when it came to promotion. In fact, in the most senior management positions those individuals of Germanic and Anglo-Saxon backgrounds predominated. Other factors of an informal kind that Dalton found to be significant were membership of the local yacht club and being of Republican political persuasion.

While no claims are made here for representativeness, this study is important in that it does suggest that informal factors can be important in career development. While it is difficult to assess the pervasiveness of these informal factors, it is undoubtedly the case that when objective qualities are present in equal proportion, then the informal factors will come into play. There is also the suggestion that in some occupations, where there are no strictly defined prerequisites for career development, then informal factors will assume greater importance. It will be shown that those occupations that are organizationally-bound will be less open to the influence of informal characteristics than those occupations that have an inter-organizational character.

A popular tradition in contemporary sociology stresses the meanings structures that individuals apply to a social situation. This social action perspective is important in presenting the individual's own definition of the situation. Using such a notion, it is clear that the definition of career success has an immediate relevance to the present discussion. Schütz (1967) has argued that any social situation and piece of social action has both a subjective and an objective meaning structure. In the case of career, we have a good example of this bifurcation.

In occupations with clearly defined structures in terms of career development, the objective definition of career success is clear. Thus, in occupational terms, a doctor who rises to the consultant level in the profession could objectively be defined as having a successful career. Certainly this is the definition that the lay public would place upon the situation. But what of the individual in a particular occupation? It is highly problematic that his definition of career success will coincide with the so-called objective definition.

As an example, a study by Pellegrin and Coates (1957) suggests that individuals' career success definitions tend to change over time and that they are rarely in accord with the 'objective' definition. The actual operation of such changes arises through changes in the individual's goals—as these change, so too do career expectations and definitions. The authors found that business executives defined career success early in their careers in terms of prestige, authority and high income. With time this definition changed in the direction of satisfying higher order needs such as self-fulfilment in work, job satisfaction, and so on.

Vertical and horizontal mobility

Indirectly, much of the above discussion has been referring to mobility of one kind or another. Although it is normal to think of social mobility as mobility between different generations, in the discussion of career movement it is necessary to restrict the discussion to one generation. Thus career mobility relates to a person's own working life. It is convenient to think of two kinds of career mobility—vertical and horizontal.

Vertical mobility is as the name implies movement (upward or downward) through a status or prestige system. This kind of mobility can arise in various ways as Caplow has delineated (Caplow, 1954, p. 59). The most obvious kind of vertical mobility occurs when there is a change of occupation which simultaneously involves a change in social rank. Obviously this kind of mobility can be both upward and downward. Vertical mobility also refers to the situation where an individual is promoted or demoted within the occupation he is pursuing. Third, vertical mobility occurs even when the individual does not change either his occupation or his level within an occupation. More status may accrue to an individual merely because of seniority in a particular occupational position, seniority which arises from length of time in a particular position. This involves a change of status. Lastly, there is vertical mobility of the kind usually referred to by sociologists—that is, mobility of an intra-generational kind as viewed from the relationship of occupational status between father and son, for example. Caplow also makes the point that from time to time an occupation *per se* can shift in the degree of status that is afforded it and this could be viewed as a further example of mobility, certainly for the occupational incumbents. While it is certain that occupations such as social workers and nurses have *in toto* increased their upward mobility in the past few decades, it would seem more appropriate to regard this as an example of occupational change, rather than as a specific example of mobility.

Horizontal mobility occurs when there is a change in occupation or job within an occupation that does not entail a change in status. As with vertical mobility there are specific kinds of horizontal mobility. In the first place there may simply be a change of job, but within the same occupation. A manager may move from production to sales or a doctor from hospital work to general practice. In these cases, mobility takes place, but there is the possibility that no change in status is involved. There may also be horizontal mobility when an actual change of occupation takes place. We can refer to the situation as one involving horizontal status when the new occupation is at roughly the same status level as the old one—the actual determination of occupational status is discussed in a later chapter. A third type of horizontal mobility refers to the case where no change in status occurs in comparing the occupational levels between generations.

Viewing mobility in terms of changes of status as an important element in the analysis of career can be further understood by reference to the empirical research that has been conducted. Two studies, in particular, illustrate the nature and the extent of mobility. Lipset and Bendix's study (The Oakland Mobility Study) has become something of a classic in the field (Lipset and Bendix, 1952). They report on the work experiences of 935 people who were the chief wage-earners in their particular families. As in the distinction made above, Lipset and Bendix found that changes in job within the same occupation were far more common than the phenomenon of changing the occupation itself. As might be expected, those individuals who did change their jobs frequently were also more likely to change their occupation more often than the less mobile. The researchers found a correlation between occupational status (as an occupational group) and the amount of mobility experienced by an individual. Thus, professional employees were the most stable, with 70 per cent of them spending around 80 per cent of their work lives in the one occupation. At the other extreme, those in unskilled occupations were the most occupationally unstable.

Further findings from the Oakland Mobility Study are that in general the range of occupations that individuals may experience in their work lives may be quite large, but that the range will be restricted to certain categories. Thus for manual workers, they tend to remain in the manual category during their work lives and similarly for white collar employees. Lipset and Bendix did find situations where the general pattern did not apply. First in the case of some individuals who predominated in manual occupations, but had experienced non-manual work. Here the latter was mainly in small businesses, low level white collar work and in sales work. The second case was those who predominated in non-manual occupations but who had spent some time in manual occupations as well. Typical of such people were the owners of small businesses who may have had their manual experience early in their working lives and then only for a relatively short time. In general, however, the study does show how little changing of occupational situation from manual to non-manual and vice versa there actually is.

The second study which lends some empirical support to the discussion of mobility and its relationship to career is Blau and Duncan's research on status mobility (Blau and Duncan, 1967). The main emphasis of this piece of research was on inter-generational mobility, but important factors relating to career mobility can be gleaned. The research was carried out in 1962 and from the study it is possible to ascertain the extent of individual mobility from first job through to the job held in 1962.

Supporting the Lipset and Bendix findings, Blau and Duncan's data show that the majority of self-employed professionals in 1962 had started their work lives as either a self-employed or salaried professional. As a further indication of this, 79 per cent of the self-employed or salaried professionals in 1962 had been self-employed professionals in their first job. These findings show very clearly the low probability of movement from this occupational level, as was suggested by Lipset and Bendix earlier. In the case of other occupations none of the figures is so prominent in displaying this feature. For example, in the case of those who were managers in 1962, only 5 per cent had started their work lives in this occupation.

Taking those in manual occupations, the craftsmen in the sample were most frequently found in unskilled or semi-skilled first jobs and thus displayed some vertical mobility during their work lives. Of those who were described as manufacturing operatives in 1962 nearly one third reported that they had started work in the same occupational category. Of those who later became operatives, they normally started work in either semi-skilled or unskilled occupations. It is interesting to note further to this, that of those individuals who were classified as labourers in 1962 over 20 per cent of them had started work in the operative category. For them, therefore, there had been a measure of downward career mobility.

The only group to approach the professionals in the degree of stability that they displayed in their careers were farmers and farmhands. Three-quarters of the farmers in 1962 had started as either farmers or farm labourers and over a half of the farm labourers in 1962 had remained in that position all their working lives.

The clear profile of occupational mobility that is suggested by the Blau and Duncan data is that at the extremes of the occupational hierarchy (professionals and unskilled workers) there is little mobility into these categories. Between them in the middle ranges of craftsmen, salesmen and manufacturing operatives (together with all the other occupations that band into this range) there appears to be a relatively high amount of mobility into the occupations represented.

Organizational careers

A distinction was made earlier in the chapter between the individual career that a person follows which may involve movement between jobs in the same occupation and those careers which almost necessarily involve remaining within the same organization (and simultaneously the same occupation, of course). Rather than encounter the familiar sociological problem of reification, it is important to stress that careers are properties of individuals. That is, a career cannot exist without an individual. But it is also important to show that certain occupations do have specific 'career lines' (Slocum, 1966). For Slocum a career is a specific associate of a complex organization, particularly since it *normally* involves movement hierarchically through a formal structure and that this movement is largely dependent upon expertise and experience (although Dalton's study discussed earlier does suggest that other issues may enter into the situation).

There are problems in seeing career lines in this way. In the first instance, the emphasis seems to be primarily on work organizations that have a bureaucratic structure (the term bureaucracy is being used in the strict sociological sense). An occupation that is situated outside the confines of a bureaucracy may also display strong career lines. The case of the medical general practitioner, who although formally a part of the National Health Service and subject to bureaucratic control from it, indicates that there can be a strong career line. It was shown earlier how the lorry driver displays a characteristic career pattern, but often the occupation is carried out in a small entrepreneurial setting where the idea of a bureaucracy would be most inappropriate.

Nevertheless, the notion of strong career lines operating within the confines of a complex organization does raise some interesting questions. Discussing the case of professionals in particular, Gouldner (1957) distinguished two polar types of latent identity of individuals in an organizational setting. These he labelled cosmopolitan and local. Briefly, the cosmopolitan displays little loyalty to the employing organization, has a high commitment to his specialized role skills and has an outer reference group orientation. Conversely, the local is very loyal to his employing organization, has little commitment to his professional skills and has an inner reference group orientation. In the context of the present discussion we are therefore presented with dichotomous career orientations of professional or organizational on the part of the individual professional. While these issues will be discussed in more depth in Chapter 5, it is crucial to mention them here since it is important for an organization to contain a balance between those individuals who display a cosmopolitan identity and those who display a local identity. Clearly, each complements the other, but the appropriate balance is crucial for the activities of the organization. The problem only arises, though, because of the organizational mechanisms that enable there to be a strong career line for some individuals. While it is important for an organization to have some stability and continuity which can arise from low turnover, if there is an excess of individuals who adopt a local orientation a certain stagnation is possible within the organization.

Career expectations

It is generally agreed that the control that professional associations exert over their members arises, in part, from the fact that during the training period for professionals, standards of professional conduct and etiquette are internalized. Thus, the profession itself is able to exercise considerable control. More than this, however, is the fact that professional members are imbued with specific expectations, not only relating to how they should behave as professionals, but also expectations relating to the development of their careers. While the literature is far from clear on this issue, it can be assumed that expectations concerning career development for manual workers exist and that they are a powerful motivator for occupational behaviour.

It is often the case that the expectations that individuals hold concerning their present and future occupational activities are inconsistent with the expectations that the reality of the situation presents. Such an inconsistency is important to recognize because of the implications both for the individual and for the employing organization.

Pavalko (1971) has referred to this phenomenon as 'career crunch'. The sources of it are many and varied. In the first instance, the period of occupational choice referred to in the previous chapter may not be as rational as certain parts of the discussion have suggested. In many cases, individuals enter an occupation with a large degree of ignorance concerning the possible outcomes. In such a state of ignorance it is highly likely that the subsequent reality will be incongruent with the held expectations. In this particular case, it is probable that the individual will embark upon a new career, since the reality is likely to manifest itself very quickly. Another source which has more far-reaching implications particularly for the individual is when changes occur in the activities of the occupation. Changes in occupational activities do occur frequently as a result of changes in technology or the development of subspecialisms within the occupation. Clearly in a situation such as this the individual is faced with a dilemma. He has been trained to work in a specific sphere of competence, which then changes for whatever reason. The individual is then at least in a position of dissonance because of the confused expectations or at most in a position where redundancy is likely. Whichever the case actually is, the individual normally needs to make radical adjustments to his occupational life in order to cope with the new situation.

Since the majority of occupations take place within the structure of a complex organization it is worthwhile discussing the situation that often arises where an individual is recruited into the organization in order to fill a specified role (all of which is entirely consistent with the individual's own expectations), but then it becomes clear that the individual could perform a different role within the organization more effectively. Here is the classic case of the organizational expectation being out of tune with the individual expectation. Of course, in many cases the individual may be content to have his organizational role redefined, but in those cases where he is not, there is a very real example of career crunch. At this point, the individual has to decide whether to stay or leave. In many cases the decision to leave may be the right one in that another organization could employ the individual in the role that he defines as appropriate.

Often it is a pointless exercise for the individual to change organizations in an attempt to maintain his occupational role definition. This is because many occupations are specific to certain organizations so that if practices change in one organization then they are also likely to change in another.

In addition to the occupational and organizational constraints that may affect the expectations an individual has of his career, personal changes within the individual can have their effects. As an example, the influence of ageing can be examined in terms of its influence on individual careers. This analysis of careers has viewed them in processual terms and since time is an essential element of the process the problem of ageing is indistinguishable from some of the career problems that are likely to occur.

Where careers take place within the structure of a complex organization there are usually formal and informal rules that govern the pace of progression of an individual through the bureaucratic hierarchy in pursuing his career. Grading employees on the category of age is a common phenomenon. While such a hierarchical system is rational in that those of greater age are deemed to have acquired more experience, the system is also a reflection of the idea that age and deference can be associated. Furthermore, age and authority are common associations. Such associations, however, may have little relationship to rationality, but may merely reflect established and accepted mores within a particular culture.

The nature of the task itself is closely related to age in many occupations. In the case of coal mining, for example, many miners may start their careers working underground engaged on such tasks as clearing roadways or operating conveyor belts. From this stage they may move up to the coal-face itself and thus be engaged on a task which is the most rewarding both economically and socially.

However, age takes its toll and a large number of miners, through age, sickness or accident, are unable to continue to meet the arduous demands of the face and withdraw to tasks elsewhere underground or to the surface itself. Here is a clear example of the relationship between age and the nature of the task. However, it should be noted that withdrawal to less arduous tasks in the case of the coal miner is not seen as career failure. This is such a common occurrence that it almost appears to have norms defining it as being appropriate.

But there are examples in some occupations where carrying out certain tasks at certain ages would be defined as inappropriate and equally strong norms to those described above could come into play. In very formal organizations, for example, such as the civil service or the military, not to have achieved a specific rank by a certain age would be defined as an unsuccessful career and is almost a way of those in super-ordinate positions within the organization displaying personal failure to the individual.

Norms such as these, whether they prescribe failure or confer the *status quo* on the individual, are obviously an important dimension in understanding the notion of career. Indeed they aid the sociological task considerably in that they enable predictability and some explanation of the issue. If an individual's age and occupation are known it is possible, within defined limits, to predict his status within that occupation. Briefly, it is known that movement through the occupational hierarchy with age is a common characteristic in most professions, in those occupations that are organizationally-bound and in a large number of white collar and craft occupations. But age in such occupational categories enables the individual to display his expertise and specialized knowledge and it is normally on the basis of these characteristics that upward mobility occurs. In the case of the semi- and unskilled worker, age brings about upward movement more for the reason of seniority than the fact that special skills have been displayed.

Conclusions

The view taken here has been that the notion of career is applicable to a wide variety of occupations and is not restricted merely to white collar occupations as the term generally implies. The main criterion appears to be the strength of the occupation and its organization. For the maintenance of the occupation it is clear that there should be stability in terms of membership. An occupational career can provide this.

An equally important function of a career is the security it brings to the individual. If it is known that there are specific hierarchical stages in an occupation then the individual is liable to render greater loyalty to that occupation. In addition to the personal satisfaction this affords the individual, it also enhances the stability of the occupation itself. Nevertheless, this situation can have its dysfunctions as the discussion has shown.

An analysis of occupational mobility has been coupled with the discussion of career since the latter normally involves the former. Horizontal and vertical mobility have been distinguished in order to illustrate the changes that may arise as an individual pursues his occupational career.

4

Occupational ideologies and status

Two closely connected aspects of occupations are examined in this chapter—their ideologies and their status. These aspects are connected in that the influence of an occupation upon the lives of members of that occupation extends beyond the influence upon a man whilst at work. The life of any individual in employment is more or less influenced by the fact that he has one occupation rather than another. It is influenced by the traditions of the occupational group itself and by the imposition of specific taboos and constraints which limit the real or supposed consequences of the behaviour which would occur if these were violated. Furthermore, the influence of the occupation is even more intrusive on the individual since occupations tend to be ranked in a social hierarchy, dependent upon the extent to which the role of the occupational member conforms with the dominant values of the society in which the occupation is carried on. Occupational status then, together with occupational ideology, is an important factor in the appeal of an occupation and is thus a potent force in recruiting and selecting people for the occupation.

To speak of an occupation possessing an ideology has an air of reification about it. The expression therefore requires some explanation. Mannheim (1936) has argued that studies concerning ideologies are essentially studies in the sociology of knowledge. By this he means basically that the ideas, the beliefs, the attitudes or the values of any individual or group need to be examined in the context in which they are to be found. So it is, Mannheim argued, that ideologies are products of the social environment and can only be understood by reference to this environment. Further, any social or political action by the individual or group is a reflection of the predominant ideology of that individual or group.

Taking this Mannheimian perspective enables us to examine the notion of occupational ideology in a non-reified sense. Earlier chapters have made it clear that occupations can be specified on the basis of their particular activities. Thus if each occupation can be said to have its own specific activities, then following Mannheim's reasoning, each occupation should develop its own ideology, or certainly the membership of a particular occupation should.

Since the nature of occupational tasks varies considerably throughout any industrialized society, it follows from the above discussion that there will be many different types of ideology within such a society. It is interesting to note that one of the main heuristic devices for assessing social class is occupational category and that broad occupational ideologies correspond roughly to social class categories. This is not to say that there will not be differences of values and beliefs between occupational members who are, say, in semi-skilled occupations, but these differences will be marginal compared to the differences between this category and, say, professional workers. It can therefore be argued that in industrialized societies there are differing patterns of ideology between different occupational groups and that these roughly equate with social class differences.

While it is difficult to talk of the homogeneity of ideology within a particular social class grouping, it is equally difficult to conceive of ideological homogeneity within one particular occupation. Differences associated with intellect, geographical area or the degree of social mobility tend to make the search for occupational homogeneity a useless quest. With this being the case, it is little wonder that the task of seeking class homogeneity is impossible.

A further aspect of any discussion of ideology relates to the individual definition of the situation. It may be possible to assign individuals to particular social classes on the basis of their occupational title—this would constitute an objective criterion. But when it comes to the question of a particular occupational and/or class ideology, then much of this is subject to the individual interpretation of the situation. Thus, the individual subjective meanings need to be considered.

The fact of significant variations between occupations by their belief systems, value patterns and overall ideology suggests that occupational ideologies can be examined as an important component in understanding the social environment in which work is undertaken. A useful schema for understanding occupational ideology variations has been presented by Dibble (1962). Ideologies can be described as parochial or ecumenic. In the case of the former, such ideologies are specific to a particular occupation. For this reason it is impossible to generalize about them in terms of a wider relevance. Dibble has suggested that most occupational ideologies are of this type. The other type—ecumenic ideologies—have a meaning beyond the particular occupation. In this sense, they can be associated with the prevailing ideologies of other occupations and with large sections of the social structure. Another important characteristic that can be associated here is the degree of complexity of the occupational ideology. It follows from Dibble's analysis that parochial occupational ideologies are relatively simple in form, whereas ecumenic ideologies are far more elaborate and complex.

While these and other dimensions obviously aid the explanation of the variations in occupational ideologies, Berger (1964) has argued that there is normally a common feature of these ideologies. This basic element is that the ideology enables an interpretation of the specific occupational activity. In turn, this interpretation provides a feeling of worth in the occupation by the occupational members and the public. It is a common observation, for example, that individuals tend to enhance their own occupation rather more than non-members of the occupation do. Pavalko has suggested that this phenomenon is both provided for and facilitated by the occupational ideology (Pavalko 1971).

An occupational ideology, therefore, serves an important function in enhancing the status and prestige of occupational members. The ideology also provides a justification for the area of activity the occupation has defined as specific to it. Indeed, the ideology often provides meaning to the activities of those individuals in the occupation where otherwise there could be none. In these terms, occupational ideologies are clearly important in understanding the social context of the work situation.

Occupational ideologies by type of occupation

Caplow (1954) distinguished four occupational types to illustrate the aspects of occupations he was interested in. Following Caplow, these four types can be used in order to analyse how ideologies vary between different occupations.

1 The professions: as Chapter 6 shows, in the case of the professions it is often difficult to distinguish sharply between work and non-work spheres of life. This extension of one sphere to another is reflected in the ideologies that surround professional occupations. Norms are laid down by the professional community that guide the individual practitioner in his behaviour, both in the work situation and outside it. In this case the occupational ideology lays down norms which are exacting for the individual. The norms inherent in the professions are transmitted to the individual initially during the lengthy training period. After this period there is continual reinforcement of the norms through constant contact with other professionals who are members of the same association and through the pursuit of a professional career.

2 The crafts: compared with the professions, those individuals who pursue craft occupations have fewer chances of occupational and social advancement. Furthermore, status achieved through the occupation is attained early in the occupational career. But compared with those occupations lower on the social scale, craft occupations do have significant amounts of status associated with them. From this point of view occupational norms exist to confer, confirm and reinforce status upon occupational members. It must be stressed, however, that this is nowhere as strong a process as is found in the professions. Similarly, as there are norms guiding the occupational conduct of professions, so among craft occupations there are rules, procedures and guidelines. Caplow has suggested that these are distinctive in the contractual obligations that are laid down defining a fair day's work, the jurisdiction of the craft and so on.

3 Factory trades: at this level the notion of a specific occupational ideology is considerably weaker. The occupation, through any association or group pressure, is unable to exert control over its members outside the work situation. Part of the reason for this is that members of the particular occupation tend to be far more transient and mobile than is the case in craft occupations and more especially in the professions. Even in the work situation itself, the occupation may find it difficult to exercise much control over its membership by means of appeal to an ideology. Trade unions, which in many instances are not occupationally based but are general unions, appear to take the place of the professional association for the professional employee. In the case of the factory

worker, however, there may well be specific attitudes and belief systems which strongly influence the behaviour of the individual and the work group whilst in the work situation. But in this case the influence arises purely from the nature of the task and the reward systems being applied and not from any internalized norms which are defined by an association and which are transmitted during the period of training.

4 The shopkeeper: the majority of self-employed people do not have occupational associations that provide guidance for behaviour either in the work situation or outside it. But behaviour is controlled by self discipline. In the same sense that Marx was able to argue that the peasants cannot be defined in class terms because of their geographical disparateness, so too with the self-employed in industrial societies. No consciousness of a collective kind develops and with that there is a lack of an occupational ideology. This is not to say that individual attitudes and beliefs cannot be shaped by the work situation for the shopkeeper and those in similar work situations. If a consensus viewpoint were to exist that represented the self-employed, the probability is that this would arise through coincidence and not through the indoctrination or conditioning mechanisms of a formal occupational association.

Occupational ideologies—an example

Management provides a useful example of the way in which an occupation has attempted to develop a specific occupational ideology and of the way in which this ideology affects the behaviour of occupational members both inside and outside the work situation.

The debate concerning management particularly in Britain and the USA has centred around two issues. First, the question of what has happened to managerial ideologies resulting in structural changes with the separation of ownership from control in private industry and second, the impact on managerial ideologies as management has attempted to professionalize itself. It will be argued that these two issues are virtually inseparable and can therefore be discussed simultaneously.

The question of whether managers can be regarded as members of a profession is an old one as is the general ownership/control debate. McIver was arguing in 1922 that managers did not have occupational associations that had any effect beyond the employing organization, even though as a group managers did possess a degree of expertise and attempted to adhere to a general code of ethics. McIver argued that the crucial element in distinguishing professions from non-professions was the extent to which the occupational group could exercise control over the standards of behaviour of the membership. From this point of view, he makes the familiar philosophical distinction between the 'will of all' and the 'general will'. The former was held to apply to managers and the latter was viewed as an essential characteristic of a profession, but which was absent in the managerial occupational group.

The distinction here then is between a prescription by a professional group of the behaviour of individual members in relation to the outside clients and the prescription of the group as a whole. Both of these elements in the distinction are crucial in understanding the development and maintenance of an occupational ideology. Through this distinction McIver argued that a definite line could be drawn between the professions and the world of business. The latter, at the time he was writing, did not possess an ethical code based on altruism, but one which emphasized the pursuit of personal interests. Even where a body of ethics could be seen, the principles were not mandatory for the individual practitioner. Indeed, no enforcement agency existed for this purpose.

Taking a different point of view, Talcott Parsons (1939) argued that there were similarities between management and the professions. Both displayed what he termed functional specialization, universalism and rationality. Parsons makes the point that even though the manager may display certain aggressive features through such things as advertising and ensuring that there is payment for all their activities, this does not deny professional conduct. Thus, Parsons argues, it is merely that the professional such as the doctor is unable to carry out such practices because of the existence of an ethical code.

In considering occupational ideologies Parsons makes some interesting points in his discussion. It is sterile, he says, to distinguish merely between the nature of the type of interest being pursued— whether altruism or self interest. Rather, it is more profitable to examine the problem longitudinally and also from the point of view of those defining the situation for themselves. So it may be that the professional and the manager are orientated towards the goal of personal success, even if the means of achieving this goal differ between them. Parsons seems to be arguing that there is a very thin line between the inability of doctors to engage in commercial advertising of their skills and managers being engaged in dishonest or corrupt practices.

It has been argued above that the development of a strong occupational ideology appears to be associated with the extent to which there is a strong occupational association that can provide norms guiding members' conduct in and out of the work situation. It will be recalled that at the time of McIver's writing, he suggested that a barrier to professionalism and presumably to the development of a strong ideology was the absence of occupational associations for management. Since that time a large number of associations have developed amongst and for managers. It is interesting to note, however, that the development of such associations has been at the expense of 'management' as a unitary body or occupation. All kinds of specialization have taken place within management and with each specialism appears to go a specific occupational association. To talk of management as an occupation therefore seems difficult. On the other hand, the developing strength of unitary occupational associations in management discussed below may suggest attempts by an expanding occupation to secure power advantages independently of any real change in the pattern of specialization.

The development of management associations in Britain can be sketched in order to illustrate this point. The Institute of Industrial Administration was established in 1920 as a response to pressure on industry for greater production following the First World War. This institute was concerned primarily with specialist practices in management such as organization and methods, accounts and works management—all areas which later split from management proper. The IIA was far from an overwhelming success and found itself with membership and financial difficulties. As the First World War had provided a stimulus for the growth of a management association, the Second World War again promoted the call for renewed strength.

In 1943 the IIA was asked for its ideas for promoting the development of British industry after the war by the Board of Trade. Two major proposals were put forward. First, the formation of a strong management association and second a research organization to carry out fundamental research into management problems. Unfortunately for the IIA, the Government committee considering the issues took these points but instead of suggesting the strengthening of the IIA, recommended the formation of a new association, the British Institute of Management. The IIA continued to function for a few years, but ultimately was forced to merge with the BIM.

The establishment of the BIM was crucial for British management. Recent years have seen attempts by managers to act 'professionally' in that a function is performed for society and society in rather an abstract way is defined as the client. This, of course, is closely analogous to the case of the pure scientist who would also argue his case in terms of a societal client. Society, in its turn, has responded by investing in management training and associated with this has imposed some restriction of entry into the sub-culture.

While the BIM does not possess a strict code of practice that governs members' behaviour it is undoubtedly true that the institute has carved a niche for itself as the occupational association for the occupation of management. Following the general discussion concerning ideologies above, it should follow from this that a specific managerial ideology should correspondingly develop.

On the question of an occupational ideology for managers, Child (1969) has argued that control over managerial behaviour has come from pressure outside the occupation (such as government) rather than from demands from within. In the work situation itself, social responsibility appears to be a key ethic which guides managerial behaviour. But this notion of responsibility is as likely to arise from self-interest on the part of managers as from a desire to behave responsibly following altruistic principles. So, without going into the debate over the differences that may result from a separation of ownership from control (and even whether such a separation has actually occurred) it is sufficient to say that for the entrepreneur any belief system that guides his behaviour is unlikely to be much influenced by strong occupational pressures. On the other hand, the non-entrepreneur in a managerial position is likely to have been trained in management at a business school or its equivalent and to be a member of an occupational association (British Institute of Management, Institute of Personnel Management, etc.) and that his behaviour is more likely to be governed by reference to the occupational body. In his case, more control will be exerted over his behaviour by the occupation and therefore, following previous reasoning, he is likely to be influenced by an occupational ideology both in the work and non-work situations. Also, referring back to the earlier discussions, for those individuals in management who are controllers rather than owners of the capital and resources, membership of and identification with a definite occupational grouping provides an opportunity for status enhancement. Indeed, Miller and Form (1964) in their study of business ideology found top managers in the USA to represent a very conscious group who perceived large differences between themselves and the rest of the population. Their self defined qualities of managing and organizing ability were viewed by them as special characteristics that demarcated them in this way.

This discussion of occupational ideologies and their influence leads directly to the related notion of occupational status—what it is, whence it is derived and the influence it has over the occupational and non-occupational lives of members.

Occupational status and prestige

That occupations are differentially rated in terms of the status and prestige accorded them is a common observation in the vast majority of societies. The reasons for the differentials and the criteria upon which they are based have been a source of sociological dispute for many years. Status stratification is very different from class stratification. The latter is based principally on an assessment of objective economic position, whereas the former is often based on non-economic considerations and in any case the gradations between the different strata tend to be much finer. Even within a particular stratum in status stratification there is likely to be differential status between those individuals in that stratum.

The criteria that have been used for assessing status differentials between occupations include such disparate items as income, the rights associated with the occupation in question, the nature of the work undertaken within the occupation according to whether it is manual or non-manual or whether it is clean or dirty, light or heavy work. Again, in everyday life there is a tendency to divide occupations on the basis of the style of dress of the members of the occupation. These widely differing criteria for assessment give some idea of the problems inherent in discussing occupational status.

These various criteria have been used to a greater and lesser extent in the many attempts by sociologists to assess occupational status. Two criteria stand out above all others in these attempts— the individual income and the level of educational attainment. Consistently, it has been shown that these two individual characteristics are correlated with the status afforded an occupation. This is not surprising since both of them are contributors to occupational status in that educational attainment is often the main criterion for admission to an occupation, and of course income, for the majority of the population, is derived from their occupation anyway. Rather than discussing the many scales that have been devised to measure occupational status, it seems more productive, in the first instance, to attempt to account for status differentiation by occupation.

Even though it can conclusively be stated that there are differential economic and non-economic rewards associated with different occupations, the reason why this should be has not been definitely agreed upon by sociologists. Davis and Moore (1945) attempted to account for the status differentials by arguing that some occupations are functionally more important than others. Also, some occupations require a longer training period than others, they involve greater sacrifices and much longer periods of education on a full time basis. Furthermore, there are differences between occupations in terms of the attractions that the tasks have to offer. A complex society has to achieve a wide range of functions and tasks and for some of these there are simply not enough people to fill the important tasks. Hence, they argue, some occupations have to be differentially rewarded.

A view of status differentials such as this was bound to promote strong reactions. The critics of Davis and Moore have argued that the functionalist argument used is extremely conservative. Furthermore, while there may be a system of differential rewards in some occupations for a period of time, what happens in practice is that the rewards continue to be received long after the functional requirements of the task have been met. While there are rather obvious criticisms that can be levelled at the Davis and Moore thesis it is perhaps significant and symptomatic of the inherent difficulties of accounting for differential occupational status.

What is clear is that in industrialized societies membership of most occupations is a process of achievement rather than ascription. Certainly, different rewards are required to recruit individuals into different occupations, in the first instance. The social organization of society defines certain occupations as having more importance than others. Therefore, social and occupational organization need to come together in order to ensure adequate recruitment into all occupations. This argument differs from that of Davis and Moore, since here the reward associated with an occupation is defined merely in terms of a sufficient one to induce individuals to enter and remain in the occupation—it is not that there must be sufficient reward to reflect the inherent worth or value of the occupation.

Occupational status is obviously important to the membership of any occupation. Not only does it comprise a reward, it also presents a goal for the individual. This is consistent with the strong societal norm of achievement. We have already seen that occupational status is a powerful motivator when it comes to individual career mobility, it has obvious effects on individual aspirations and the general motivation to work.

Caplow (1954) noting that an individual's social status is largely determined by his occupation, has suggested three factors which are central in understanding the general phenomenon of occupational status. First, industrialized societies have seen the withering away of many informal groupings in favour of formal ones, partly as a result of rapid growth. The development of the large complex organization sees individuals often referred to by their position in the organization rather than by reference to the individual himself. And the experience of urbanization stresses segmental rather than total role relationships. All of these characteristics, Caplow refers to as aggregation. Second, and closely linked to the first factor, there is occupational specialization on a large scale. With specialization, the attributes of each position become more abstract, particularly to the lay community which again emphasizes the reference to occupational and/or organizational title. This process of differentiation to which Caplow refers also promotes strict authority systems. Third, is the process of rationalization, the gradual removal of informal and primary mechanisms of control and the introduction and substitution of formal controls of behaviour.

According to Caplow these general trends of aggregation, specialization and rationalization have the effect of placing greater emphasis upon the occupation that an individual is engaged in, from the point of view of assigning status. This proposition can be examined in the light of some of the important studies that have been undertaken to assess empirically occupational status and its importance.

Possibly the most widely quoted study of occupational status is that of the American National Opinion Research Center (NORC) published in 1947. The study is important because of its wide sample covering a large cross section of the American population and because its specific aim was to discover some of the basically held opinions about occupations and their status. A detailed description of the methodology of the study is unnecessary, except to say that respondents were required to choose a statement that corresponded to their own feelings about a checklist of ninety occupations.

Taking the notion of a status hierarchy related to occupations, the NORC study found that respondents, in compiling their hierarchy of the occupations presented to them, placed emphasis upon training and the degree of responsibility in the occupation in areas of public welfare. It is interesting that even in a country such as the USA which displays such heterogeneity on several dimensions, throughout the country there was general agreement by respondents for the general order of the ranking of occupations. Regional differences were present, such as respondents in the north-east of the country placing greater status on professional and semi-professional occupations, but differences of this kind tended to be rather slight. Coupled with these regional differences were the differences that could be associated with size and type of community. It was found that small rural areas tended to overrate the visible occupations such as farmers and postmen (overrating here means compared with the national average rating). Likewise, respondents from large urban areas placed greater emphasis upon more esoteric occupations which included titles such as creative artists, scientists and bar tenders.

As the discussion concerning occupational ideologies mentioned, there is a tendency for people to enhance their own occupations when asked to evaluate them. This finding is supported by the NORC data. Also the only real difference in ratings between men and women (and then they were small differences) was the fact that women rated the 'liberal' occupations higher. Examples would be teaching, social work, general service occupations and religious occupations. The other personal characteristic making for general differences in the ratings was the level of educational attainment.

Mention has been made of the factors the respondents considered important in compiling the occupational hierarchy. In evaluating individual jobs two factors were frequently mentioned—high income and a contribution to the needs of society. Needless to say, the low income groups in the sample placed more emphasis upon high income than did those in relatively high income occupations.

Using a smaller sample the 1947 study was replicated in 1963 in

47

order to assess the amount of change that had occurred over the intervening time period. It is most interesting that virtually no change could be recorded in comparing the two years. In fact the correlation coefficient between the two sets of scores was 0.99, an exceedingly rare figure in the social sciences. The overall correlation, however, does disguise some slight changes within and between groups. For example, the 1963 figures display a slightly higher rating for manual workers and a slightly lower one for the semi-professionals. Nevertheless, the overall score remains very significant. The NORC researchers also attempted a comparison between the 1963 figures and the earliest figures available which dated back to the mid 1920s and again, overall, there was no significant change in the hierarchical structure of occupations.

Strictly speaking the NORC studies were measuring occupational prestige and not occupational status. Sociologists normally make a distinction here in that occupational status gives an indication of the education and income that are associated with a particular occupation. On the other hand, occupational prestige is the evaluation of an occupation by a number of people. In other words, status has more of an air of objectivity about it while prestige relies for its measurement on subjective interpretations.

Comparisons between measures of occupational prestige and status indicate that prestige is a far more stable phenomenon than status. Taking the American situation, it is clear that over the period between 1925 and 1963 there had been large changes in both the education and the income associated with various occupations. And yet, the NORC study indicates that the public evaluation of these occupations had not significantly altered. From this point of view it can be argued that occupational prestige is more stable than status.

In Britain, the evaluation of occupational prestige and status has followed similar lines to the American studies. Most of the social status studies have taken occupation as the chief determinant. For example, the Registrar General classifies social class through a five point schema and also uses a sixteen point classification of socio-economic groups. The most widely known and used study of occupational prestige in Britain is that of Hall and Jones (1950). Like the American NORC study respondents were asked to evaluate a list of occupations in terms of a ranking system. Hall and Jones found that there was a general consensus in the actual social grading of the occupations between the respondents. The greatest variation in response came from those respondents experiencing the lowest occupational prestige. This last point has been found to occur in other studies. The study by Young and Willmott (1956) which attempted to grade manual workers socially found that manual workers produced much variation in their assessments. This arose, they found, because respondents tended to grade occupations according to their definition of usefulness to society. In this sense, it was often the case that manual workers were placed higher on the scale than non-manual workers. This tends to reiterate the point made earlier concerning the subjective meanings that individuals attach to social phenomena.

Studies concerned with measuring occupational prestige clearly have drawbacks associated with them and their value can be seriously questioned. For example, Parker *et al.* (1972) observe that respondents are asked to make judgments and distinctions that they do not make normally. Furthermore, prestige scales infer that occupations can be rated in a uni-dimensional way. Such an inference is questionable.

Recent sociological research into occupational prestige and status has attempted to overcome the difficulties inherent in the traditional studies. Attempts have been made to measure status and prestige in a non-evaluative manner and also to get away from the idea of viewing the concepts purely in a hierarchical form. Such attempts have started their analysis through the use of the concept of occupational situs.

Occupational situs

A situs is a category that is placed at the same level as other categories such that all categories are given equal evaluations. The idea of an occupational situs was first used by Hatt (1950). His argument for introducing the concept was based on the kinds of inadequacies that we have already seen in the measurement of occupational prestige and status, in particular seeing the occupational structure of a society in hierarchical terms and also the problems associated with people ranking a large number of occupations in a way they had probably not thought of before.

Hatt used the 1947 NORC data and found that some occupations could be construed into one scale and others into different ones. He suggested that it would be better to think in terms of occupational families or situs categories with each category containing broadly similar occupations. He discovered eight situs categories—political, professional, business, recreation and aesthetics, agriculture, manual work, military and service. In this way, it seemed to be feasible to compare occupations within situs categories such as those occupations placed firmly in the military or in business, but it made little sense to compare occupations which belonged to different categories. But there are problems here because of the status differences that appear between the different categories (compare for example professional with agriculture) and the basic principle of situs categories is that the categories should have similar evaluations.

Hatt's work is important because of the work it has since generated by other researchers. For example, Morris and Murphy (1959) produced a typology of ten situs categories comprising legal authority, finance and records, manufacturing, transportation, extraction, building and maintenance, commerce, aesthetics and entertainment, education and research, and health and welfare. The main criterion underlying each category is the function for society of a particular activity and that each activity is equally necessary for the functioning of society. Therefore, as each category has a necessary function, the occupations within each situs category contribute to this function. The empirical validity of the approach of Morris and Murphy has been tested by Pavalko (1971) who concludes that there still seem to be problems associated with whether the categories can be equally evaluated or perceived by respondents. In spite of this, the situs concept in discussing occupational prestige and status is important. The fact that the type of work can be assessed is a significant development and will no doubt generate interest in similar types of research.

One further feature of occupations that research into situs categories has not fully explored is the fact that within a particular occupation there will be differential status and prestige. The discussion of careers made it clear that often the occupational organization produces this differential. Taking the extreme example, in the professions it is stated that professional members occupy a theoretically equal status position with their colleagues. In practice, a pecking order develops based, not on differential specialized knowledge necessarily, but on grounds of seniority and reputation within the profession. A similar position has been noted in the case of manual occupations with age and seniority being the source of the intra-occupational status differences.

It will be recalled from the discussion of occupational ideologies that the belief systems that are generated through the work situation are often carried over into the non-work situation. The likelihood of this occurring, it was suggested, varies with the strength of the occupation and its corresponding association. A similar situation pertains in the case of occupational status, particularly for those individuals who derive high status from their occupations. Parker *et al.* (1972) have referred to a 'portable' status, i.e. one's occupational status can provide entries into institutions and activities in the non-work sphere. However, this is not a universal phenomenon as the discussion concerning work and leisure will show. In many cases the worlds of work and leisure are totally separate and work status appears to bear little relationship to status outside work.

Conclusions

A recurring theme in this book is the influence that occupations have upon the non-work lives of occupation incumbents. The two aspects of occupations examined in this chapter give some idea of the strength of this influence. By taking the view of ideologies as socially derived phenomena the development of specific occupational ideologies has been noted together with the way that occupation members are influenced by them in all aspects of their lives. In addition to this, ideologies have been seen to be closely related to the status and prestige afforded an occupation. The specific example of the development of management in the UK illustrates the relevant points well.

Occupational status has been shown to be closely related to the overall social status that an individual possesses. American studies have shown the slow tendency for prestige ratings to change over time, even though the more objective assessment of status changes rather faster. Because of some of the inherent difficulties involved in measuring occupational status and prestige the notion of situs categories has been introduced. While there has not been a large amount of research into this notion, it does hold the promise of overcoming some of the measurement problems of status and prestige.

5

The professions

Of all the different aspects of occupational sociology that can be delineated, studies of the professions seem to have attracted more sociological research than any other. Any discussion of the professions must therefore explore at the outset why this should have occurred. Possibly the most important reason is that of all occupations, it is the professions that have grown in size and importance the most during the course of the present century. Significant changes of this kind must have important effects upon the social structure and upon the non-professional occupational sector. In other words, the growth of the professions can be examined as part of a social process and as such has attracted the interest of the sociologist.

As an example of the changing proportion of professionals and of professions, the figures extracted from census material by Halmos (1967) can be examined. Taking England and Wales and attempting to make some allowance for classification differences, Halmos compares the years 1901 and 1961. In 1901 there were 53.7 people per professional worker compared with 24.5 in 1961. The absolute increase in the numbers of professionals can be seen from the two censuses. In 1901 there were 606,260 professionals in England and Wales compared with 1,880,090 in 1961. This represents a percentage increase of 484.

Such a rapid growth raises obvious sociological questions, in particular what is the nature of the professions themselves, how do occupations turn themselves into professions, what has happened to the traditional status of the long established professions, is the term profession any longer a meaningful one to use when so many people claim to be professionals, can the theory of élites be applied to the professions any longer? Issues such as these give some explanation of why it is that a distinct sub-specialism within sociology concerned exclusively with the analysis of the professions has emerged. The breadth of these questions also illustrates the difficulties of doing justice to 'the sociology of professions' in a volume of this size.

Instead of attempting a summary of the large literature concerned with the professions that is now available, it would seem more fruitful to take a limited number of the issues that are of concern to the sociologist of the professions. This task is made relatively easy since there is a high level of consensus among sociologists as to what are the crucial issues. The dissensus arises over the interpretation of the issues.

The definition of professions

When the word profession is used in a strict sense, particularly by the layman, it is those 'traditional' professions of law and medicine, those well established professions of accountancy and the church that spring to mind. While it is true that such professions did constitute the chief types at the end of the last century and while they did possess a number of common characteristics or traits, it is no longer valid to refer specifically to these as 'the professions'. So what has happened to account for the development of new professions and for occupations to be vigorous in their attempts to professionalize themselves?

The main factor that accounts for the rise in the number of the professions and simultaneously of professionals is the specialization that is characteristic of industrialized societies. The so-called traditional professions developed specialisms within themselves which eventually developed into new professions in their own right or were subordinate to the traditional profession. Parallel to the growth of specialization has been the technological change which again is characteristic of industrial societies. The growth in the number of professional engineers and scientists illustrates this point.

But having established that specialization and technological developments gave rise to many of the emergent professions during this century still leaves the definitional problem.

Millerson (1964) has adequately raised the issue of the problem of definition. According to Millerson, three problems create difficulties in arriving at a definition. First, there is a semantic confusion. A problem such as this is common in the social sciences, but the term profession seems to have attracted a very wide variety of lay meanings. The distinction between a professional and an amateur is commonly made, someone who is paid for what he is doing is often referred to as a professional and again the term is sometimes applied to all those people who work in white collar occupations. While there is this kind of confusion in terms of calling some occupations professions when they clearly are not, at the other extreme is the practice of *not* referring to some occupations as professions when there are good grounds for doing so. The public image of the librarian or the engineer is such that the layman often does not recognize professional status here—the librarian being perceived as the individual who stamps his books and the engineer is the person who repairs his car. Clearly, there are differences between the sociologist's and the layman's use of the term professional.

The second problem distinguished by Millerson refers to what he calls structural limitations. The many volumes written about professions seem to agree on the kinds of traits that professions need to have in order to distinguish them from the non-professions. These traits which include a theoretically based skill, an ideal of service, an adherence to the professional code of ethics and so on (see p. 55 below for a more detailed discussion) do seem to hold for those occupations to which sociologists would ascribe professional status, but the important question is whether it is necessary for all professions to possess all of the characteristics, and if not, how many is the absolute minimum for a profession to be said to exist? Questions such as these lie in the path of arriving at an agreed-upon definition.

The third issue is referred to by Millerson as the dynamic realism of the situation. Because we tend to think of the traditional professions in the first instance, there is also the tendency to think of the social attributes and norms that tend to be associated with them. For example, there is the tendency to regard only independent practitioners as true professionals, that there should be a close and intimate professional-client relationship guided strongly by a code of ethics and that the mere existence of a professional association will ensure appropriate control over the behaviour of members and that this association will be the main body to award the licence to practise.

These three general problems concerned with the confusion over the term profession are themselves significant if only because they give an indication of conceptions of occupations and professions as they are popularly held. Indeed, they also indicate something of the perception that some occupations have of themselves. But for the sociologist they are problems that need to be overcome since they do produce confusion over what specifically is being talked about. A simple way out of this confusion is to examine what sociologists tend to agree are the major characteristics of a profession. In other words, to examine traits, in spite of some opposition for this approach (Johnson, 1972).

Those occupations that sociologists and others agree can be labelled professions do appear to hold a number of characteristics in common. It has been shown that there is some doubt over how many occupations can be called professions and which they actually are; it is nevertheless possible to distinguish a minimum list of necessary attributes or traits. What such a list does, in effect, is to demonstrate that the professions are merely a special type of occupation, an extreme type lying at the extreme end of a continuum with unskilled manual work being close if not actually at the other end. Because of this notion of a continuum some of the professional characteristics are shared with other occupations on the continuum.

1 The activity performed must be socially required and the activity must be carried out by a group of people. The activity must also be distinct from the activities being performed by other groups of people. This characteristic is obviously one that does not distinguish professions from other occupations. But equally, it is a necessary, if not a sufficient condition.

2 Those individuals carrying out the distinct activity need to organize themselves into an association and to establish strict criteria specifying who shall be admitted to it. Again, this does not distinguish a profession from some other occupations. For example, butchers in the UK have established an Institute of Meat with laid-down criteria for admission and yet only in the extreme lay sense would butchers as a group be regarded as professionals or members of a profession. It is worth noting that the establishment of an association again stresses the differentiation of the activity being carried out from other similar activities. The difference here is that not only is the differentiation stressed externally to the public, but also internally to the occupation itself. For example,

external differentiation might involve the occupation changing its name (as with reporters being journalists) and internal differentiation displaying to the occupational membership that some members are central or leading members while others are very peripheral.

3 The occupational group develops the criteria of admission mentioned above to such an extent that admission to the occupation requires the successful passing of an examination that is deemed relevant to the activity of the occupation. In the case of the professions, such an examination normally requires a relatively high level of intelligence. Furthermore, the hurdles provided by the educational system have the function in this respect of separating out those who could or should be admitted and those who could or should not be. In the case of the professions, there seems to be an effort made to link the admission criteria with university qualifications or their equivalent.

4 It is necessary for the professional group to develop a code of ethics. This code serves two important functions, first to guide the conduct of the members of the profession and second, to form the basis for a mandate from society to pursue the specialized activity discussed above. What these two functions mean is that the member of the occupational group will provide a service to the client and that the interests of the client will be protected by the professional group itself. In the second place, the code of ethics ensures that the client's interests will be served and protected and that 'the public' is aware of this.

5 Society or the public need to support the claim for professional control of the affairs of the occupational group as a whole; that is, give support to the professional mandate. This is normally achieved by a licensing process which often has legal support. This protects the profession's area of jurisdiction and also sanctions the profession's control over members' conduct.

It is clear from these five characteristics that a profession can be distinguished from other occupations primarily on the basis of whether the client's interests are served and protected. Other classifications in the literature may have more or less characteristics listed, but the fundamental points are raised by the presentation here. In saying that the client's interests are served and protected by the profession, it could be argued that such an occurrence also arises in other occupations. However, the classification also displays the manner in which the service and protection are effected and this above all else is the distinguishing criterion.

Arising from this, it is evident that the control of the professional role is of paramount importance. This control has a number of aspects relevant to it. First, a key part of the professional role is that the professional shares responsibility with his client for the decisions that are made from the application of the professional's expertise to the client's problems. The professional therefore brings values to bear upon the problem which may or may not be recognized by the client. In this sense, the role of the professional is different from that of an agent role.

Second, the professional recognizes that applying these values is founded upon a competence on the part of the professional individual and the fact that the role demands that all other considerations (particularly the consideration of self interest) are subordinated to the welfare of the client. The definition of this situation is such as to include the bringing to bear of professional standards which are invariably written into the code of ethics of the profession. Also, it can be assumed that the client has some knowledge of these professional standards upon entering into a professional-client relationship.

Third, and arising from the second point, the individual professional must subscribe to the professional code of the profession of which he is a member. The acceptance of the code of the profession is the guarantee to the client that the professional will behave in a predicted manner. This point is of particular importance in the case of the traditional professions such as medicine and law. It is still relevant to the new and the emergent professions even where the professional acts as an employee rather than as an independent practitioner. If the professional employee is to be distinguished from any other employee of a complex organization it needs to be on the basis that he, the professional, subscribes to a professional code of ethics before entering into any contractual relationship resulting from employment. If this does not occur then he can only be labelled as an agent at best, or at worst as an employee with prescribed duties.

Most of the literature relating to the professions makes the point that an important distinction between professional members and non-professionals is that the former have the power to regulate those affairs which touch upon the affairs of the professional group. This power is vested in the professional group as a whole and therefore presupposes that the group will possess sufficient cohesiveness and solidarity to allow it to claim or exercise this power. In this way, the professional member is able to carry out his service role virtually independently of the power sources which are external to the profession itself.

But the discussion of what is meant by a profession so far indicates that the power that the profession possesses tends to be related to internal affairs rather than to external ones. So it is that the professional group is concerned with the influence of members' conduct in the carrying out of the service role and function. The profession is not concerned with the more general exercise of power within society at large nor with any attempt to regulate the affairs of others. While a mandate is necessary for the profession to function and while this mandate seeks to influence 'society' at large, the influence attempts that are made are primarily designed to secure the mandate so that in turn the profession can regulate its own affairs. Once this mandate has been secured the professional group would terminate any more general attempt to influence.

The last chapter showed that the professions (that is, those occupations that meet the requirements listed above) do have a relatively higher status in society than other occupational groups. Furthermore, they are accorded higher prestige by members of society. They tend to have a higher standing (socially) than the other occupational groups and the granting of a mandate to the professional group to control its own internal affairs on behalf of society is both a cause and an effect of this higher social standing. High status is normally associated with high influence and so it needs to be recognized that although social influence on the external situation is not a necessary part of the process of achieving professional standing, it is often a part of the process of actually carrying out the professional's role in society. In this sense, there is something to be said for regarding the professions as part of the social élite.

Science as a profession—an example of the professional process

Some suggestions for the rise in the number of professions and professional workers have already been made. The process of specialization and a changing technological situation accounts for the development of science and with it the associated professions. Carr-Saunders (1933) makes the point that professions such as engineers, chemists and physicists arose as a response to the progress of science as a whole and to the mechanical revolution.

It seems therefore that science has provided a basis for the development of a number of professions and the question of whether it is itself a profession is far more problematic. In fact, science is probably better viewed as a situs category as a professional family, rather than as a profession in its own right. After all, science is not an activity that is desired by society as such. Rather, science is a means of achieving or approaching some socially desirable activities. Wilensky (1964) has suggested that the functional equivalent of the professional's service ideal distinguished above is the scientist's disinterested search for truth. But only if the work of the scientists is defined in this abstract way could there be a technical basis for an activity.

Connected with this is the problem of who comprises the clients of science. In the strict sense there is no client except perhaps society. But this is again an abstraction in that it suggests that society desires that someone pursues the truth and therefore provides a licence to a group of people to do this. Again, there is the question of to whom is the scientist accountable? Whatever service the scientist renders to society is rendered by the individual through the community at large.

There are probably scientists whose actual role in society satisfies these criteria. But in the same way that science provided the motivation for the establishment of specific professions in the nineteenth century so now the scientific approach promises to generate a number of separate professions in which there is a recognizable activity and a determinate client and/or employer. Since a large proportion of those engaged in scientific pursuits work in an applied field, this suggests that there is a major differentiation within the science profession as a whole.

Once the activities of scientists can be identified it then becomes possible to recognize both the clients and the employers other than the rather nebulous 'society at large' notion. The specific contributions of scientists may in fact derive from the pursuit of truth in situations where there are bounded activities and where there are recognizable intermediate agents between the scientists and society. Indeed, there is every reason to suppose that the disinterested scientists who apply their science to the discovery of truth at all costs are a rare category found predominantly in academic institutions. Further, there are good grounds for believing that the remainder of the scientists are to be found in clearly demarcated occupations in the context of complex organizations wherein both the clients and the employers can be identified. A distinction therefore seems possible between the industrial scientists and the guardians of the science professions.

In making this distinction, two things follow. In the first place, the so-called guardians tend to be more vocal in stating the employment conditions for scientists. In the professional pecking order, the guardians are the leaders of the profession, their role is to represent the overall profession's basis for a claim for a societal mandate. The scientist's competence and his disinterest guarantee a service to society. But equally, society has to permit the control of entry to the professions by the professions themselves on the basis of examination and to provide the condition of freedom regarded as necessary for the discovery of truth.

The second implication of recognizing an internal differentiation of activity within science is that the expanding subordinate section, such as the industrial scientists, is likely to express a desire for independent professional status. In the same way that medicine developed a large number of differentially rated professions over the course of the last hundred years, so science could be expected to do likewise.

Any occupation undergoing a process of expansion is likely to produce a level of insecurity for its members and one solution to this is the formation of a strong and stable occupational association. Caplow has pointed out that in the case of manual occupations undergoing expansion, there is normally a tendency towards the development of a craft organization. For white collar occupations, the tendency is for the occupations to attempt to professionalize themselves (Caplow, 1954). But Caplow is of the opinion that there are indications that most non-routine white collar occupations are in the process of professionalization. This would seem to be rather a dubious proposition.

In the case of scientists, those who work in industry probably do press for professionalization of their distinguishable occupations. In the early stages of this process it is necessary for the occupational practitioners to come from outside the occupation proper—in this case from the generic occupation of science. But it is also interesting to speculate on the attempt by the central members of the science professions to develop the ideology of science in the face of the underlying changes in the directions of application of their acquired intellectual technique. The 'scientist' could be expected to react to these in some way. If science can be regarded as an expanding occupation then the scientist would be expected to comment on the suitability of people other than scientists to make the required contribution.

The professional in the organization

That changes have taken place in the character of the professions and of professionals themselves in modern society is not a novel observation. Changes of this kind have been monitored by sociologists for some time now. For example, Weber, in noting that the dominant type of administrative structure at the time of his writing was the bureaucracy, also observed the development of what he labelled the collegial form of administration (Weber, 1947). By collegial, Weber was referring to the administrative organization that catered for the needs and demands of professional employees.

Basically, the changes that have occurred in complex organizations during this century from this point of view are that the salaried employee has increasingly been employed in the large complex organization. As the discussion above has indicated, it is felt that the professional is an independent fee-receiving individual, but the picture in modern societies requires amendment because of the changes that have occurred during the past fifty years or so. It is now typical to see the professional as an employee, whether he be a professional engineer, a medical practitioner, an accountant or a social worker. That such a change has occurred requires an explanation and further, requires analysis of how complex organizations and the professions themselves have adjusted to these changes and the sorts of structures that have resulted.

The most important difference that can be observed where professionals are employed in large numbers in complex organizations is that to secure compliance, different types of authority and control are employed. Whereas the bureaucratic model of organization would suggest that the authority is derived largely from the position of the role incumbent in the organization (Dunkerley, 1972), the professional model of organization suggests that authority is derived from being a member of a profession. For instance, Blau and Scott (1962) in analysing the nature of professional authority and control have noted that control arises in the first place from the long period of training undergone by the professional. This training period ensures that the professional not only acquires specific expertise but also ensures that the code of ethics, which to a large extent guides the subsequent conduct of the professional, is internalized. Control also arises, they note, from the supervision of the professional peers. It is these who ensure that standards are maintained, who can pass professional judgments on their colleagues and who can impose disciplinary measures where necessary. Now, authority in this situation is clearly very different from that which obtains in the bureaucratic organization where the source is basically the position of the role incumbent in the hierarchy of command. Thus, it is direction from above which is the hallmark of the bureaucratic situation compared with direction from self-control and colleague-control which characterizes the professional organization or the organization that employs professionals (at least for those professionals in the organization).

However, it is rare to find a totally professional organization. Most organizations employing professionals display elements of a bureaucratic structure as well. This fact has led many sociologists to indicate the problems inherent in such organizations. In the context of the present discussion, the chief difficulty lies in the fact that the professional working in the complex organization is subject both to control from his colleague group and from his position in the organization. The dual nature of this authority could lead to psychological and social problems for the professional, excepting the fact that mechanisms do exist which enable the professional to come to terms with his environment. The important mechanism of relevance here is the degree to which the organization member who is a professional turns either to his employing organization or to the profession of which he is a member.

The literature is redolent with the processes involved in this adaptation to the environment by the professional and various concepts have been employed to describe this process. For example, Reissman (1949) has coined the term the 'functional bureaucrat' to describe the professional who turns to his employing organization as the source of control and yet maintains some contact with his professional association outside the organization. Again, Wilensky (1964) has used the term 'professional service expert' in his study of intellectuals in trade unions to refer to those who are not too concerned with the labour movement *per se* and would change their employment if they could better employ their specialist skills and expertise. In other words these people would turn to their profession rather more than to the employing organization as an escape from the potential marginality of the role. As a last example, Hughes (1958) has described as 'itinerants' those people who turn more to their professional group than to the employing organization, who are prepared to move between organizations in order to improve their professional standing.

It is clear then that a variety of attempts have been made to describe the phenomenon of professionals in complex organizations. But the most systematic of these attempts was that made by Gouldner in two articles published in 1957 and 1958. Reference has already been made to this work in Chapter 3. In the first instance, Gouldner was concerned with the incidence of conflict in complex organizations, not only between individuals, but also within individuals. This led him to describe what he called the latent social roles of organizational members. As we saw in Chapter 3 three variables were distinguished as being of importance for analysing these latent social roles: loyalty to the employing organization; commitment to specialized or professional skills; and reference group orientations. On the basis of the analysis of these variables, Gouldner was able to hypothesize two latent organizational identities—cosmopolitan and local. Taking the three variables listed above, Table 1 shows the two latent identities.

Table 1

	Cosmopolitan	Local
Loyalty	low	high
Commitment	high	low
Reference group	outer	inner

Returning to his initial interest in the analysis of conflict within organizations Gouldner pointed out that organizational problems can arise from these two latent identities. In the first place, when people are being assessed in a relatively bureaucratic fashion they are being assessed on definable criteria such as their skill or competence in the job, the amount of training and experience they have received, and so on. It is rare indeed for a factor such as loyalty to be employed in such assessments. This leads to organizational problems when a factor such as promotion is being considered.

However, the concepts of cosmopolitan and local are very general categories and have little heuristic value as they stand. Gouldner was aware of this problem and attempted some refinement of the concepts. An empirical study of an educational organization confirmed the predictions relating to cosmopolitanism and localism. By themselves, however, the concepts are quite sterile, they tell us little about the problems of professionals in organizational employment. The empirical study did, in fact, suggest that three behaviour forms were associated with the concepts: differential patterns of participation; differential propensities for rule tropism; and differential degrees of influence within the organization.

In brief, what the findings indicated were that the influence increased along the scale from cosmopolitan to local; that locals participated far more than cosmopolitans (although there was even more participation at the intermediate points of the continuum); and locals tended to be higher on rule tropism than did the cosmopolitans.

The academic research that has followed Gouldner's original exposition has tended to support his findings (cf. Blau and Scott, 1962; Kornhauser, 1962; Pelz and Andrews, 1966). Consistently it has been shown in these studies that it is very rare for professionals in complex organizations to be orientated both to the profession of which they are a member and to the employing organization of which they are also a member.

An inconsistent finding was discovered by Bennis *et al.* (1958) in a study of nurses in an outpatients department. Here, those nurses that had a professional orientation did not appear to show a more cosmopolitan orientation, certainly in terms of their degree of commitment to the employing organization. Some qualification of this finding needs to be made. As Blau and Scott point out, in this situation there could have been a conflict between commitment to professional skills on the part of the nurses and the opportunities for advancement in their profession. In the case of nursing, advancement often means giving up nursing skills because of the greater administrative component of more senior roles.

In a later study, Glaser (1963) analysed the supposed conflict of orientations of professional scientists in a research organization. Here, he could find little evidence of the predicted conflict. This is something of a deviant case since a conflict between professional goals and organizational goals could not be described realistically.

In this case, both were orientated towards the discovery of new scientific knowledge.

Taking up this point, Thornton (1970) has argued that the amount of a professional orientation in an organization and in the organizational involvement of members may determine the inconsistency between the two sets of interests. He found that in some circumstances the commitments of the professionals themselves and of the organization may be compatible. The crucial factor, as Thornton saw it, was the degree to which the professionals both perceived and experienced the organization following the principles of professionalism—the two are not necessarily mutually exclusive. But in the short run professionals may experience satisfaction with given conditions, whereas in the long run the professional who is totally committed to the ideals of the profession could well find the situation frustrating and one which imposes severe limitations on professional advancement.

Miller and Wager (1971) have attempted to explore the constructs further by introducing the notion of socialization. Adult socialization may account for the differences that can be observed in role orientations and this may take the form of professional or organizational socialization. The findings of the study carried out with professional engineers and scientists in the American aerospace industry suggest that the different orientations to be found were largely a result of differences arising from the type and length of training of the professionals. The scientists, it was found, were more cosmopolitan than the engineers and these orientations were reinforced by the organization. In terms of Gouldner's original interest in the area—conflict—it was found that there was very little conflict because the expectations of the professional employees were consistent with the reality as found in the organization, particularly from the point of view of the career system.

The last of the empirical studies to be referred to is that of headteachers in British secondary schools carried out by Hughes (1973). This position is one of a classic nature with the professional adopting a largely administrative role. Hughes found that the heads could be classified in the same way that Gouldner had done. For cosmopolitans, Hughes substituted the term innovating heads and for locals he used the term traditional heads. He showed that those who were more professionally orientated were expected to give more encouragement to innovation within the school situation. Those members who provided this encouragement were also found to be more tolerant when the head had to apply bureaucratic methods (such as the meeting of deadlines). The suggestion here is, therefore, that while the professional may actually denigrate administrative and bureaucratic techniques from a sentimental point of view, when it comes to it, he may well accept the administrative responsibilities that are associated with the role in the organization for what they are. This point has been well demonstrated by Warwick (1974). He has suggested that professionalization and bureaucratization need not be viewed as mutually exclusive qualities but that on occasions there is a degree of interpenetration. This may be little more than the professional 'using' the bureaucratic system, but nevertheless there is a degree of usage made of it, regardless of motives.

The organizational professional has not only had his effects upon the professions and the orientations of professional members. Recent decades have also seen organization structures themselves being altered to accommodate the professional employees. The result has been the so-called professional organization as typified by the hospital or the social service department in local authorities. This model of organization rests upon the same foundations as the legal rational bureaucracy, but is distinguished in terms of the organization of its resources for the purpose of dealing with complex and unstructured problems. Associated with this is the fact that the distinguishing characteristics of the professional organization are congruent with an acceptance of authority which is based upon the specialized and certified knowledge of highly trained members of the organization. This may have much in common with the authority base in bureaucracy, but it is a special case of this at least, in that the level of knowledge involved is much higher and the authority is not regarded as concentrated at the centre, but dispersed through all members who have knowledge.

Complex professional organizations usually contain two elements. First, the groups of professionals or near professionals whose members' status within the group is theoretically equal, but actually unequal on the basis of seniority or reputation. Second, the work-task groups which bring together different professionals in the solution of problems (for example, doctor, plus nurse, plus clerk, plus porter) but again with a definite order of precedence which would, for example, put the doctor over the nurse. Within this framework negotiations take place. The framework has a professional base with representatives having other professional bases which might, as occasion arises, have more or less given authority. In this sense, to think of a professional organization solely in terms of equality amongst its members with virtually no hierarchical structure is erroneous. Nevertheless, it is clear that adjustments have had to be made to the bureaucratic form of organization to accommodate professionals working in the organization. Therefore, in addition to organizations modifying the traditional concept of the profession, the professional employee also modifies the organization to the extent that, as Warwick (1974) argues, a certain professionalization is taking place within organizations and a certain bureaucratization is taking place within the professions.

Conclusions

It is perhaps significant that the professions should have attracted such a large amount of interest from sociologists. The review of the salient points presented in this chapter must of necessity be merely a brief and possibly partial summary. Criticisms of the approach taken could be levelled from several points of view. However, the chapter has attempted to describe what the sociologist understands by the term profession and the idea of the process of professionalization. It is in the nature of the discipline that not all sociologists would agree with the descriptions presented, but the analysis of the scientist as professional does shed light on the difficult issues involved.

The other area discussed covering the organizational professional may well reflect the biased interest of the author, but notwithstanding that this issue is of fundamental importance in understanding the contemporary workings of the professions. Furthermore, it highlights related issues such as the problems of organizational careers discussed in Chapter 3.

6

Occupations and their non-work effects

In the course of the text so far there has been frequent reference to the fact that occupations have effects on the non-work life. Discussions about occupational status, career and professionalism all indicate that occupations do have important effects on the individual beyond the time that the individual is actually in his work role. Some of these effects can now be explored in more detail. In particular the influences of occupations on the family, on the degree of community involvement, on political behaviour and on the general category of leisure will be analysed. Such an analysis will reveal the pervasiveness of occupations in relation to the individual.

Occupations and the family

The main impact that occupations have upon the family is through membership of a social class, which is largely determined through occupational status. It is difficult to separate out the effects that social class membership has on the family from the effects of occupational status. In this sense, the task of examining the relationship between occupation and family is made that much simpler.

An interesting relationship that is of interest to sociologists as well as the layman is the degree of overlap that exists between work roles and family roles and the extent to which the status and prestige which are accorded an individual at work carry over into the family situation. The sociological interest in this relationship arises because there appear to be distinct differences according to the level of social class. Parker *et al.* (1972) in discussing the relationship point to the fact that the greater the degree of commitment to the work situation the less the commitment to the family. The social class differences are such that in the middle class situation, the social position of the family is very dependent upon which occupation is being pursued by the husband. In spite of this close relationship, there is relatively little chance of the wife being able to identify totally with the husband's occupation because of its relative complexity. This is not likely to be the case for the working class occupation, but here the occupation does not bestow high status outside the work situation.

A study by Blood and Wolfe has distinguished three patterns of types of relationship between the husband's occupation and the wife's role. These are collaborative, supportive and peripheral. Typical examples of these three would be the wives of farmers being collaborative, the wives of many white collar workers and professionals being supportive, and the wives of manual workers being peripheral (Blood and Wolfe, 1960).

Similarly, in examining the attitudes of men to their occupations in terms of the extent to which they have aspirations to succeed, some interesting patterns in terms of the effects on family life emerge. A study by Edgell (1970) analysed this in terms of middle class spiralists. By spiralists is meant those who progress through their careers with associated geographical mobility. For those respondents with a high aspiration to succeed, work was their central interest in life, they had segregated work-family roles and tended to be dominant in family relationships. Those with a medium aspiration separated their interests between work and home which produced role conflict for them which was often manifested in inconsistent family relationships. Lastly, for those with low aspirations, the home was the central life interest, joint roles could be observed and egalitarianism in terms of family relationships.

Our analysis of occupational choice revealed that the visibility of occupations plays a large part in how wide the choice is from which an occupation is selected. The role of the family in this process is self evident. A degree of socialization into the world of work takes place in this way. But the more general process of child socialization is related to the occupational position of the father, in so far as the quality of child socialization varies by social class.

Of recent changes that have occurred in the family, the increased employment of women in the labour force has had one of the most profound effects. It has already been pointed out that women comprise roughly one third of the labour force in Britain and that nearly two thirds of these are married. Considerable amounts of socio-logical research have investigated the possible effects of this, parti-cularly on the effects of the wife's employment on relationships within the family.

The most obvious effect that the employment of married women has is to make these women more economically independent. It would seem logical to argue that more equality in the making of decisions that affect the family should ensue. However, there is some evidence to suggest that there are differential effects by social class. Nye (1963), for example, found that there were more adverse and negative effects on the relationship where the husband was in a low status occupation, compared with the situation where the husband was in a relatively high status one. The underlying prob-lem that arises in examining this relationship is that the motivation for married women working has to be accounted for. If the decision is made purely from choice, the effects on family relationships will be different from those where the decision is made through econo-mic necessity.

Occupations and community involvement

Before examining the extent of community involvement on the part of individuals from different types of occupations, it is worth-while also examining the relationship between occupations and the community. While this is done more systematically under the sub-heading of leisure patterns, the broader influences can be looked at here. At one extreme is the relatively closed community which is dominated by one industry. In this situation the status accorded individuals at work will be carried over into the community situ-ation. For example, in an unpublished study carried out by the author and his colleague, G. Mercer, of a traditional small mining community in the north of England, it was found that the hier-archical pattern of relationships found in the work situation was sufficient to demarcate relationships in the community. The felt unease of relationships between miners and overmen and deputies was carried over into the community and those with status and prestige in the work situation also enjoyed the same in the com-munity. Furthermore, the elected leaders at work such as shop stewards were significantly more active in the community than the rank-and-file.

But a traditional mining community displaying a certain degree of social and geographical isolation is an extreme form of community. Far more typical is the urban industrial community. Even here though, the pattern exhibited in the mining situation is to be found, although in a less extreme form. For example, Mogey (1956) has described the effects of the development of the motor industry on the city of Oxford. In the context of the present discussion, Mogey found that the traditional patterns of informal hierarchies of jobs among manual workers were broken down by the changes, particularly those changes which led to Oxford becoming a relatively affluent city. Indeed it can be hypothesized that the impact of various attributes of mass society has altered many attitudes and behaviour relating to occupational life.

As another example, Elizabeth Bott's study of urban families showed that the intensity of a family's neighbourhood network depended much on the husband's occupation. Where work-mates were also neighbours, then the network was found to be localized. A loose form of network was found where colleagues did not live in the neighbourhood (Bott, 1957).

In terms of community involvement, a useful measure is the extent of membership of voluntary associations. Sociologists generally agree that there is a direct relationship between membership and participation of voluntary associations and occupational status. Taking a National Opinion Research Center (NORC) study reported by Hausknecht (1964) it was found that the degree of participation was 53 per cent of professionals and managers, 41 per cent of clerical and sales workers, 32 per cent of manual workers with varying types of skill, and 21 per cent for labourers.

In addition to this direct relationship, there is evidence that indicates that the degree of involvement is partly dependent upon the nature of the occupation as well as its level in the status hierarchy. Hagedorn and Labovitz (1968) showed that the occupational role predisposed individuals towards certain community activities. Those individuals whose work roles involved isolation tended to have a low degree of community involvement compared with those in work roles associated with creative work involving features such as problem solving and decision making. It was demonstrated that the work role had these consequences rather than providing evidence of an explanation in terms of personality type.

The evidence presented here would suggest that there are clear differences in the amount and quality of involvement in community affairs by type of occupation. This is contrary to the argument put forward by some sociologists which suggests that there has been an increasing homogenization of the population in terms of their social activities. Part of this 'convergence' argument was tested by Goldthorpe and his colleagues using a sample of affluent workers (Goldthorpe, Lockwood, et al., 1967). Not including trade unions the average number of formal organizations belonged to in the community by the sample was less than 1½. For the manual workers' wives the number averaged out at ½. While these figures are themselves low, the point is reinforced since the organizations belonged to were predominantly working class organizations such as working men's clubs and angling clubs. It was clear that movement into the more middle class community associations was not taking place. The affluent worker sample was not located in a typical working class community with strong extended kin ties and yet kin and neighbours still played a large part in the non-work lives of the sample. Such evidence lent support to the contention that the process of 'embourgeoisement' was not occurring. And for the purposes at hand it does suggest that occupational role is a determinant of the degree and type of community involvement.

Occupations and political activity

There appears to be a clear relationship between the status of an occupation and the voting behaviour of those actually pursuing that occupation. It is a commonplace observation that in Britain the Conservative Party represents the middle class and the Labour Party represents the working class or that in the USA the Republican Party reflects the views of the white collar worker and the Democratic Party represents the manual worker. However, in the case of the American political system such a generalization does not have the same level of validity as in Britain because of the greater heterogeneity of American political parties.

In Britain the national figures suggest that around two thirds of manual workers vote for the Labour Party, while around three quarters of white collar workers support the Conservative Party. Such figures have remained consistent over most of the general elections since 1945. Such a fact lends further support to the argument that a process of 'embourgeoisement' has not taken place in British society. Again, taking data from the study by Goldthorpe and his colleagues, of the manual worker sample 71 per cent reported that they had voted for the Labour Party in the 1959 election and that 69 per cent had been regular Labour voters since 1945 or from whenever they had first been eligible to vote.

At a different level, it is interesting to note that there is not the same clear relationship between occupational level and active involvement in politics. Butler and Pinto-Duschinsky (1970) have shown that in the 1970 British parliament only 26 per cent of Labour members came from manual occupations. Of course, this is consistent with the discussion in the previous section concerning the low level of involvement in formal organizations in the non-work situation of those in manual occupations.

Returning to an earlier discussion where the concept of occupational situs was introduced, it will be recalled that situs categories appeared to offer a useful analytical framework for understanding various aspects of occupational life. Murphy and Morris (1961) examined the relationship between situs categories and political affiliation. Taking the four categories of commerce, finance and records, manufacturing, and building and maintenance clear differences in party allegiance were observed. Even when income and educational levels were held constant the relationships between situs categories and party identification remained.

Occupations and leisure

In this section it is proposed to examine the relationship that exists between work and occupations and leisure. Defining what is meant by leisure is difficult mainly because of its subjective characteristics. Parker (1971) has made the point that leisure also has a certain normative component in that individuals tend to define it in terms of what they think it ought to be and not necessarily in terms of what it actually is. Even thinking of leisure as the time when an individual can do what he wants is rather unsatisfactory since for those in particular occupations, the boundary between work and leisure is a very fine one. Indeed, it is often left to individual interpretation in deciding the line between work and leisure. While this is the case for only a minority of occupations, it is important to recognize that it is a contrivance to discuss leisure without relating it to work.

Work and leisure do comprise different sets of activities, but these activities are closely related. In the case of work, activities are goal orientated and the demands placed upon the individual are normally demands from an outside agency. In the case of leisure, the activities are decided by the individual himself. Any control there is upon the individual can be manipulated by him in the leisure situation. This implies that there is freedom in leisure that is not present in work.

What is put into the work situation by the individual is something that has an economic or social value for others, in the leisure situation the in-put has more of a value for the individual himself. Work tends to have an instrumental character as compared with the more terminal value of leisure.

It is interesting to note that the values of 'the Protestant Ethic' still have significance in modern society. Briefly, the Protestant Ethic states that an individual's moral status is reflected in the results of work. In this sense, leisure, free time, idleness, etc., all have a negative value in that they do not contribute to the moral well-being of the individual. While such an ethic no longer has a strong influence upon the lives of individuals in industrialized societies, the underlying principles seem to have become internalized into the culture of many such societies. A manifestation of this internalization is seen in the attitudes towards leisure time. For many, there is a certain guilt about engaging in leisure activities unless leisure time has somehow been earned through having worked hard. Despite this, the predominant ethic does seem to have shifted from one with a work emphasis to one with a social or leisure emphasis.

When perceived in these ways, leisure can be viewed as a problem both for the individual and for society. It is a problem in that it is a result of technological changes in the work situation which have produced more free time for the individual. Also, there is an incompatibility between this increased free time and the internalized cultural work ethic.

Parker (1971) has argued that two dimensions are crucial for a complete understanding of work and leisure and the relationships between them. Time and activity have to be analysed. Thus, both work and leisure need to be viewed as qualities of activities that exist over time. And to refer to the discussion above, it is clear that the goal orientations of the various activities have to be understood if an understanding of work or leisure is to ensue.

The difficulties in distinguishing just what is meant by leisure as distinct from work can be observed in the work of Berger (1963). He has taken the rather normative view of what leisure should be and implied value judgments regarding what is useful leisure time and what is not. He sees a number of issues that are relevant to the analysis of leisure. In the first place there is the concern expressed by those in certain personal service occupations to ensure that the leisure activities of certain groups are fulfilling and satisfying for the members of these groups. Thus, social workers, youth leaders, clergymen and the like concern themselves with the leisure activities of adolescents, of the unemployed, of the socially disadvantaged, of the aged, and so on. From another point of view, Berger has expressed concern about the leisure activities of the cultural and intellectual élite. He observes the threat to their traditional activities arising from the mass culture that results from large numbers of people being able to afford to engage in the traditionally élite activities.

Discussions such as this tend to be strongly influenced by a normative sense of what should be the leisure activities of certain groups. Such a value-laden approach does have some significance, but for the purposes of developing or generating a theory of work and leisure that is sociologically grounded, debates of this kind do not have much promise. A more worthwhile approach to examining leisure and its relationship to work activities is to explore the different use that leisure is put to by individuals in different occupational categories.

It has been suggested that technological changes have been a major contributor in reducing the amount of time individuals spend at work. However, this is only at an official level. The forty hour week has become the standard normal working week for most occupational groups in Britain. But the contribution of overtime working has meant that the actual number of hours worked has not been significantly reduced in recent years. For example, the average number of hours worked as overtime in 1958 was only 0.5, by 1966 this figure had risen to 6 hours. During that time the normal working week had been reduced by approximately four hours. The other phenomenon that distorts the picture of a forty hour week is the extent of double jobbing or 'moonlighting'. In 1964 it was estimated that one sixth of the total working population had more than one job. What is interesting about this is the fact that the phenomenon is extensively practised across a wide range of occupations and is not restricted to manual occupations.

In spite of such obvious discrepancies between the official working week and the number of hours actually worked, if the amount of free time available is taken *in toto* then the proposition that there has been a reduction in work time in recent years does have some validity. This arises from the facts of earlier retirement and later entrance into the work force.

Pursuing the issue of free time, Wilensky, in examining the American occupational structure, has observed that there has been an unequal distribution in the amount of free time available by different occupations. Taking data since 1850, the most significant gains have been in manufacturing and mining industries and more recently in farming. White collar workers, particularly civil servants, professionals and managers, have made little progress in gaining more free time (Wilensky, 1963).

Wilensky found, through an examination of six professional groups and groups of both white collar and manual occupations, that those individuals at the higher occupational status levels worked longer hours. Wilensky reinforces the point made above that the generally held view that there have been large increases in recent years in the amount of leisure and free time available throughout the working population is something of a myth. But more than this, that what gains have been obtained have not been equally distributed throughout the working population.

Before examining what is possibly the most systematic attempt to develop a theory of leisure and its relationship to work, it is necessary to examine the kinds of leisure activities that individuals from different occupational strata engage in. In the first instance, reference can be made to the wide-ranging study carried out by Clarke (1956). Five levels of occupations were taken that corresponded to the prestige ranges and scores from the NORC study of occupational prestige in 1947 mentioned in previous chapters. At level 1 (that level accorded the highest amount of prestige) 'cultural' activities predominated in the leisure activities. Included in such activities were going to the theatre, reading, bridge, home entertainment and cinema going. At the next level down in terms of occupational prestige the predominant activities were going to parties and to football games as well as visiting friends or relations at weekends. Golf was the most mentioned activity for those at the third level. Home-based activities such as car maintenance predominated for level four. At the lowest level of occupational prestige activities included television viewing, family activities, drinking and card playing.

Analysing these activities in more detail, certain interesting patterns can be discerned. In the first instance, for those individuals at levels 3 and 4 activities of a passive nature seem to be the most dominant. Activities that involved creativity (in the sense of building or constructing or modelling something) were reflected in the leisure activities of those in the lower prestige groupings rather than in the higher ones. One further example from the study relates to what the respondents said they would do if they were given an extra two hours a day free time. Those in the lower occupational levels were more likely to state that they would relax and rest than in the higher levels of prestige. It is obvious from this study that different activities are reflected at different occupational levels and also that individuals at these different levels have differing perceptions of the meaning of leisure time. Other studies such as Gerstl's (1963) suggest that there are even significant differences between occupations even though the occupations may be at roughly the same prestige level. Such differences are due to the differences that arise in the work situations, the skills employed and the social imagery that each occupation has.

The theory of work and leisure

The most important and systematic work that has emerged on the relationship between work and leisure and on providing a theoretical framework for the analysis of the two activities has undoubtedly been carried out by Stanley Parker (1971). This section attempts a summary of his work together with some refinements that could be made.

In the first instance, Parker distinguishes two schools of thought about the relationship between work and leisure in industrialized societies—the segmentalists and the holists. The segmentalists argue that life in advanced industrialized societies can be neatly divided into two distinct spheres of activity, each of them being largely independent of the other, each having its own problems, rewards and opportunities. For example, Mann (1973) has suggested that the manual worker has been forced to adopt a dual consciousness in relation to work and non-work. For the individual, the latter have become separated. This clear separation of work and non-work or leisure largely denies the existence of any interchange of consciousness between the two sectors. Indeed, the segmentalists argue, the contemporary leisure industry is largely predicated on the existence of such a gulf (see for example the work of Dumazedier 1967).

A more popular slogan that expresses the segmentalist view is that 'leisure is self realization'.

Against this view is the argument of the holists—that work and leisure are increasingly coming together. The holists argue that it is a myth to talk specifically of leisure or free time because it is inconceivable that man can totally ignore his work experience. Equally unconvincing are the allusions to two worlds of unsold and sold time. The holists see the heightened exploitation of human resources as a growing phenomenon. This embraces both the situation at work and in leisure. Briefly, the argument states that the problems of work are also the problems of leisure. Leisure, far from constituting an escape from the pressures of work, merely mirrors these in a different context. Certainly, for some, the difficulties of work and leisure reinforce each other.

The problem with the arguments put forward both by the segmentalists and the holists is that the propositions are at a very general level and in order to examine the empirical validity of them it is necessary to look at particular occupations in some detail. This Parker did, taking the occupations of banking, youth employment and child care. It is clear that these three do not represent the occupational structure in any meaningful way, but rather they are at roughly the same level of occupational status and yet display large differences in the nature of the work undertaken. Basically, Parker was interested to discover how much importance individuals attached to work and leisure in their total lives.

From the empirical study of these three groups, two distinct patterns could be distinguished in terms of the value placed upon work and leisure. The individuals working in the banking industry experienced a complete break in their leisure period from the work situation. Leisure was enjoyed because of its difference from work. The main interest in life appeared to be the family. In the case of the other two occupational groups leisure was again enjoyed, but a lot of free time was taken up with activities associated with work. Here the main interest was work rather than leisure.

On the basis of these findings and the results from other studies, Parker suggests that three patterns of the way in which individuals relate their work to leisure can be delineated. These he calls the extension pattern, the neutrality pattern and the opposition pattern.

The extension pattern, as the name implies, arises when there is no clear demarcation between activities in the work situation from those in the leisure situation. Here the boundary between work and leisure is very blurred and work constitutes the main interest in life rather than home or family interests. The neutrality pattern exhibits some differences between work and leisure activities. As the main interest in life, work is relegated behind the family and home. In the third case—the opposition pattern—the distinction between work and leisure is very distinct. Leisure activities have no resemblance to work activities and the main interest in life is definitely to be found in the non-work world of the individual.

These three patterns clearly provide a useful typology for the analysis of the relationships between work and leisure. Each type has certain work-related factors associated with it and also some typical occupations. For those individuals displaying the extension pattern there is normally a high level of autonomy, with the neutrality pattern the degree of autonomy is somewhat less, and is lowest for the opposition pattern. Coupled with the degree of autonomy in the work situation can be seen specific types of involvement and a distinct degree of work satisfaction.

Parker suggests typical occupations whose incumbents might display the three patterns. Most professionals and some skilled manual workers are said to exhibit the extension pattern. The neutrality pattern is typical of low level white collar workers, semi-skilled manual workers and semi- or minor professionals. For the third category with the opposition pattern very routine clerical workers, and unskilled manual workers would be typical.

While there is an apparent use to this typology it does suffer from the fact of being based to some extent on *a priori* judgments. This is recognized by Parker himself in stressing the need for more empirical testing of the propositions.

The biggest problem area would appear to lie with the opposition pattern. The separation of work and non-work in the way that Parker has described is open to criticism. In the first place, the Marxist tradition places the primacy of work in an individual's life experience as central. In this sense, activities in the work situation have their effects in leisure activities. Indeed, it could be argued that what happens in the work situation spills over into the non-work sphere and unifies the individual's whole existence. Parker's argument seems to be that the leisure activities compensate for the work situation.

Hoggart's work on working class culture (Hoggart, 1958) suggests that there has been a disappearance of the traditionally working class leisure pursuits. If this is so then it entails the loss of an area where the individual could experience some possibility of self expression. Furthermore, there is a greater involvement on a mass scale in hitherto 'élite' pleasures—a phenomenon that has been held to display the basic freedom and justice of modern industrialized societies. The consequences of these developments could be that the new habits and activities in the non-work situation, far from leading to any greater self-realization, may in fact have merely served to confirm the wider loss of control of manual workers—at both work and play.

There is strength in the argument that the central life interest of manual workers lies outside the factory gates. But in one of the 'typical' occupations that Parker suggests displays this pattern it is arguable whether a distinct line such as this can be drawn. The study referred to earlier by Dunkerley and Mercer suggests that the dual consciousness proposed by Parker is not readily apparent in the case of coal miners. Similarly, there is not the strict separation in terms of work being seen as a liability and non-work time as an asset. Furthermore, it does not follow that the experience outside the pit compensates for the trials and deprivation inside.

Conclusions

In this chapter explicit reference has been made to the effects of occupations on the non-work lives of occupation members. The areas chosen for discussion—the family, the community, political life and leisure—all display a consistent underlying theme, that occupations cannot be adequately understood without reference to wider phenomena. In this chapter many of the issues of previous chapters have recurred. Here the link between occupations and society has been made more explicit.

Although there is rather a frustrating tendency for contemporary sociologists to conclude their work with a plea for more work to be done in whatever field they are studying, such a plea is very necessary here. There is no denying that a great deal of work has been undertaken to examine some of the issues discussed in the chapter, but the issues are so crucial for sociological understanding over and above the sub-discipline of the sociology of occupations that such a plea is justified in this case.

7
Summary and further reading

It was shown at the beginning of this volume that the antecedents in occupational sociology stretch back to the founding fathers of sociology itself. However, only in relatively recent times has considerable research been undertaken and theorizing developed on the subject matter. But given this comparatively recent interest it is now clear that our knowledge about occupations and society is very extensive. The sociological concern with occupations and their social effects has reached the stage where the empirical material far outweighs the theoretical substance. One very clear need is for substantive theories to be developed grounded upon the empiricism. One possible cause of this situation is the fact that American work on occupations dominates the field. This work has a distinct positivist approach. It is interesting to note that the debate concerning theories of occupational choice that has occurred in Britain (Williams, 1974) has no parallel in the American literature on occupations. Similarly, the important attempt by Parker (1971) to develop a theory of work and leisure has no American counterpart.

While the level of empirical work has been predominantly at the level of the interaction between the individual and the occupation, it is perhaps significant that there have been few attempts to produce a model demonstrating the effects of occupations in terms of the social structure and vice versa.

Increasingly, there are pressures placed upon sociologists, particularly those with an empirical leaning, to ensure that their material has a societal relevance. While such pressures may be dissonance-producing for some sociologists, it is interesting that occupational sociologists in general are becoming more aware of the need to make the material relevant. Of course, this may suggest that occupational sociologists are likely to develop a new paradigm. Such a suggestion is highly problematic, although the indications of a change in the existing paradigm are present, albeit without a new paradigm being visible.

The basic shifts in paradigm that can be discerned reflect an increasing maturity in occupational sociology. The material presented in this text provides a summary of the current areas of awareness. Some areas have been more intensively researched than others, for example, occupational choice, the professions, status and mobility. The significance of these areas of study is that they reflect the dynamics of occupations. Furthermore, such areas have a concern beyond that of the academic sociologist in that they reflect societal and pragmatic pressures for more information and for answers to questions posed by the areas of analysis.

At another level, the development of occupational sociology can be observed in terms of a response to concerns at a societal level. It is fashionable for the cynic to argue that sociologists have their eyes on the main chance, that is, in this context, that they are able to recognize social problems and areas of societal concern and thoroughly investigate them for the purposes of self aggrandisement rather than being motivated by genuine social concern. While there may be some truth in this cynical viewpoint, the claim of Gouldner (1970) that the emergence of new social problems is normally associated with a reorientation in any relevant scientific endeavour would seem to have more credence. Such a reorientation can be seen in the analysis of occupations.

Another cause of changing paradigms lies in the nature of the scientific endeavour itself. It is necessary for any dynamic discipline to challenge constantly the important contemporary trends in that discipline. Merely because an approach may be popular and has enjoyed a level of popularity for some time does not make it immune from critical appraisal. Such challenging and criticism are evident in the sociology of occupations.

As an example of the way paradigms may shift, whether as a result of societal pressure or because of healthy criticism from within the discipline or both, the contemporary concern with the nature of work in industrialized societies can be cited. It is interesting that a standard text in occupational sociology for over a decade (Caplow, 1954) should be entitled *The Sociology of Work*. An examination of the text discloses that the nature of work and its social consequences were not seen as areas of concern. The emphasis is rather more on a structural analysis of occupations and their concomitants *per se*.

The claim was made at the beginning of this volume that three basic areas are of concern to the occupational sociologist—structure, culture and change. In the course of the text the attempt has been made to reveal and answer the questions raised by these concerns. While it is possibly mandatory in a volume such as this to make apology for what at times must needs be a superficial analysis, the hope is that the general issues and problems have been raised together with some solutions. Clearly, there is a close relationship between occupations and society. For the sociologist to understand and interpret the relationship is crucial.

Further reading

Texts that cover the general field of the sociology of occupations are relatively rare and those that do exist tend to be mainly American. The books listed below adequately amplify many of the discussion points made in the present text. For more detailed references to specific areas in the sociology of occupations, the reader is advised to consult the works cited in the main body of the text and listed in the general bibliography.

Caplow, T. (1954) *The Sociology of Work*, McGraw-Hill, New York.

Hughes, E. C. (1958) *Men and their Work*, The Free Press, Chicago, Ill.

Parker, S. R., Brown, R. K., Child, J. and Smith, M. A. (1972) *The Sociology of Industry*, Allen & Unwin, London.

Pavalko, R. M. (1971) *Sociology of Occupations and Professions*, F. E. Peacock, Itasca, Ill.

Taylor, M. L. (1968) *Occupational Sociology*, Oxford University Press, New York.

Bibliography

BENNIS, W. G., BERKOWITZ, N., AFFINITIO, M. and MALONE, M. (1958) Reference groups and loyalties in the out-patient department, *Admin. Sci. Qtrly*, 2, pp. 481-500.

BERGER, B. M. (1963) The sociology of leisure: some suggestions, in E. O. Smigel (ed.) (1963), pp. 21-40.

BERGER, P. L. (1964) *The Human Shape of Work*, Macmillan, New York.

BLAU, P. M. and DUNCAN, O. D. (1967) *The American Occupational Structure*, John Wiley, New York.

BLAU, P. M. and SCOTT, W. R. (1962) *Formal Organizations*, Chandler, San Francisco.

BLOOD, R. O. and WOLFE, D. M. (1960) *Husbands and Wives*, The Free Press, Chicago.

BOTT, E. (1957) *Family and Social Network*, Tavistock, London.

BRENNAN, R., COONEY, E. W. and POLLINS, H. (1954) *Social Change in South West Wales*, Watts, London.

BUTLER, D. and PINTO-DUSCHINSKY, M. (1970) *The British General Election of 1970*, Macmillan, London.

CAPLOW, T. (1954) *The Sociology of Work*, McGraw-Hill, New York.

CARR-SAUNDERS, A. M. (1933) *The Professions*, Clarendon Press, Oxford.

CHILD, J. (1969) *The Business Enterprise in Modern Industrial Society*, Collier-Macmillan, London.

CLARKE, A. C. (1956) The use of leisure and its relation to levels of occupational prestige, *A.S.R.*, 21, pp. 301-7.

DALTON, M. (1951) Informal factors in career achievement, *A.J.S.*, 56, pp. 407-15.

DAVIS, J. A. (1964) *Great Aspirations*, Aldine, Chicago.

DAVIS, K. and MOORE, W. (1945) Some principles of stratification, *A.S.R.*, 10, pp. 242-9.

DENNIS, N., HENRIQUES, F. M. and SLAUGHTER, C. (1962) *Coal is our Life*, Eyre & Spottiswoode, London.

DIBBLE, V. K. (1962) Occupations and ideologies, *A.J.S.*, 68, pp. 229-41.

DUMAZEDIER, J. (1967) *Toward a Society of Leisure*, Collier-Macmillan, London.

DUNKERLEY, D. (1972) *The Study of Organizations*, Routledge & Kegan Paul, London.

DUNKERLEY, D. and MERCER, G. (1974) Mobile miners, *New Society*, 29, p. 85.

EDGELL, S. (1970) Spiralists: their careers and family lives, *B.J.S.*, 21, pp. 221-9.

FORM, W. H. and MILLER, D. C. (1949) Occupational career pattern as a sociological instrument, *A.J.S.*, 54, pp. 317-29.

GERSTL, J. E. (1963) Leisure, taste and occupational milieu, in E. O. Smigel (ed.) (1963), pp. 146-67.

GINSBERG, E. (1951) *Occupational Choice: an approach to a general theory*, Columbia University Press, New York.

GLASER, B. (1963) The local-cosmopolitan scientist, *A.J.S.*, 69, pp. 249-60.

GOLDTHORPE, J. H., LOCKWOOD, D., BECHHOFER, F. and PLATT, J. (1967) The affluent worker and the thesis of 'embourgeoisement', *Sociology*, 1, pp. 12-31.

GOULDNER, A. W. (1957) Cosmopolitans and locals—1, *A.S.Q.*, 2, pp. 281-306.

GOULDNER, A. W. (1958) Cosmopolitans and locals—2, *A.S.Q.*, 3, pp. 444-80.

GOULDNER, A. W. (1970) *The Coming Crisis of Western Sociology*, Heinemann, London.

HAGEDORN, R. and LABOVITZ, S. (1968) Occupational characteristics and participation in voluntary associations, *Social Forces*, 47, pp. 16-27.

HALL, J. and JONES, D. (1950) Social grading of occupations, *B.J.S.*, 1, pp. 31-55.

HALMOS, P. (1967) The personal service society, *B.J.S.*, 18, pp. 13-28.

HATT, P. K. (1950) Occupations and social stratification, *A.J.S.*, 55, pp. 533-43.

HAUSKNECHT, M. (1964) The blue collar joiner, in A. S. Shostak and W. Gomberg (eds) *Blue Collar World: Studies of the American Worker*, Prentice-Hall, Englewood Cliffs, N.J., pp. 207-15.

HOGGART, R. (1958) *The Uses of Literacy*, Penguin Books, Harmondsworth.

HOLLOWAY, R. G. and BERREMAN, J. V. (1959) The educational and occupational aspirations and plans of negro and white male elementary school students, *Pacific Sociological Review*, 2, pp. 56-60.

HOLLOWELL, P. G. (1968) *The Lorry Driver*, Routledge & Kegan Paul, London.

HUGHES, E. C. (1958) *Men and their Work*, The Free Press, Chicago.

HUGHES, M. (1973) The professional-as-administrator: the case of the secondary school head, *Education Admin. Bull.*, 2, pp. 11-23.

JOHNSON, T. J. (1972) *Professions and Power*, Macmillan, London.

KATZ, T. E. and MARTIN, H. W. (1962) Career choice processes, *Social Forces*, 41, pp. 149-54.

KORNHAUSER, W. (1962) *Scientists in Industry*, University of California Press, Berkeley.

LIPSET, S. M. and BENDIX, R. (1952) Social mobility and occupational career patterns, *A.J.S.*, 57, pp. 494-504.

MCIVER, R. M. (1922) *Community*, Macmillan, New York.

MANN, M. (1973) *Consciousness and Action among the Western Working Class*, Macmillan, London.

MANNHEIM, K. (1936) *Ideology and Utopia*, Harcourt, Brace, New York.

MERTON, R. K. (1952) *Social Theory and Social Structure*, The Free Press, Chicago.

MILLER, D. C. and FORM, W. H. (1951) *Industrial Sociology*, Harper & Row, New York. Second edition 1964.

MILLER, G. A. and WAGER, L. (1971) Adult socialization, organizational structure and role orientations, *Admin. Sci. Qtrly*, 16, pp. 151-63.

MILLERSON, G. L. (1964) *The Qualifying Associations*, Routledge & Kegan Paul, London.

MOGEY, J. M. (1956) *Family and Neighbourhood*, Oxford University Press, London.

MORRIS, R. T. and MURPHY, R. J. (1959) The situs dimension in occupational structure, *A.S.R.*, 24, pp. 231-9.

MURPHY, R. J. and MORRIS, R. T. (1961) Occupational situs, subjective class identification and political affiliation, *A.S.R.*, 26, pp. 383-92.

NATIONAL OPINION RESEARCH CENTER (1963) reported in *Opinion News*, 9, pp. 3-13.

NATIONAL OPINION RESEARCH CENTER (1963) reported in *A.J.S.*, 70, pp. 286-302.

NYE, F. I. (1963) Marital interaction, in F. I. Nye and L. W. Hoffman (eds) *The Employed Mother in America*, Rand McNally, Chicago.

PARKER, S. R. (1971) *The Future of Work and Leisure*, MacGibbon & Kee, London.

PARKER, S. R., BROWN, R. K., CHILD, J. and SMITH, M. A. (1972) *The Sociology of Industry*, Allen & Unwin, London.

PARSONS, T. (1939) The professions and the social structure, *Social Forces*, 17, pp. 457-67.

PAVALKO, R. M. (1971) *Sociology of Occupations and Professions*, F. E. Peacock, Itasca, Ill.

PELLEGRIN, R. J. and COATES, C. J. (1957) Executives and supervisors: contrasting definitions of career success, *Admin. Sci. Qtrly*, 1, pp. 506-17.

PELZ, D. and ANDREWS, F. M. (1966) *Scientists in Organizations*, John Wiley, New York.

REISSMAN, L. (1949) A study of role conceptions in bureaucracy, *Social Forces*, 27, pp. 305-10.

ROSE, E. J. B. (1969) *Colour and Citizenship*, Oxford University Press, London.

SCHÜTZ, A. (1967) *The Phenomenology of the Social World*, Northwestern University Press, Chicago.

SIMPSON, R. L. and SIMPSON, I. H. (1962) Social origins, occupational advice, occupational values and work careers, *Social Forces*, 40, pp. 264-71.

SLOCUM, W. L. (1966) *Occupational Careers*, Aldine, Chicago.

SMIGEL, E. O. (ed.) (1963) *Work and Leisure*, College and University Press, New Haven.

SPREY, J. (1962) Sex differences in occupational choice patterns among negro adolescents, *Social Problems*, 10, pp. 11-22.

THORNTON, R. (1970) Organizational involvement and commitment to organization and profession, *Admin. Sci. Qtrly*, 15, pp. 417-26.

TUNSTALL, J. (1962) *The Fishermen*, MacGibbon & Kee, London.

WARWICK, D. (1974) *Bureaucracy*, Longmans, London.

WEBER, M. (1947) *The Theory of Social and Economic Organization*, Oxford University Press, New York.

WILENSKY, H. L. (1963) The uneven distribution of leisure, in E. O. Smigel (ed.) (1963), pp. 107-45.

WILENSKY, H. L. (1964) The professionalization of everyone?, *A.J.S.*, 70, pp. 137-58.

WILLIAMS, W. M. (ed.) (1974) *Occupational Choice*, Allen & Unwin, London.

YOUNG, M. and WILLMOTT, P. (1956) Social grading by manual workers, *B.J.S.*, 7, pp. 24-33.